Journey through Jerusalem with No Hands

One Woman's Travel toward Holistic Healing

Janet Penney

WestBow
PRESS
A DIVISION OF THOMAS NELSON

WestBow Press books may be ordered through booksellers or by contacting:

WestBow Press
A Division of Thomas Nelson
1663 Liberty Drive
Bloomington, IN 47403
www.westbowpress.com
1 (866) 928-1240

ISBN: 978-1-4908-1580-0 (sc)
ISBN: 978-1-4908-1579-4 (hc)
ISBN: 978-1-4908-1581-7 (e)

Library of Congress Control Number: 2013921095

Printed in the United States of America.

WestBow Press rev. date: 11/20/2013

Dedication

I would like to dedicate this book to all the intercessors in the earth; the hidden ones of God. Those who give their lives in praying on the behalf of others. Most people do not realize the effectual power that proceeds from your mouths. No acknowledgements may ever be given, yet the world is continually reaping the benefits of your strategic prayers. Thank you for dwelling in the secret place of the Most High God.

Foreword

"I am excited that Janet has written this book. I'm sure that many will be greatly blessed by what the Holy Spirit has laid upon her heart in writing this work. Janet carries the DNA of what the Lord is doing prophetically in this day and hour. Her involvement in the house of prayer model, and her years of experience, make her a valid and a key voice the Holy Spirit is speaking through today."

Carlo Sarmiento,
Director of Orlando House of Prayer

Endorsement

"Janet's story will give you hope, courage, and the faith you need to overcome any obstacles that is standing in the way of fulfilling your God-ordained destiny. These true life events present an amazing account of the grace of God that stems from a life that is committed unto Him. I count it a privilege to have been chosen by God and by Janet to be the *hands* she needed as we walked the streets of Jerusalem together. We did not need easy-just possible. Undoubtedly, my life will never be the same. One key thing I have learned through this journey is to be very careful in what you say you want, because you just might get it!"

Louann Moore
Co-Senior Pastor, Critz Church of God
Critz, Virginia

"If you googled *Perseverance*, I'm quite sure a picture of Janet Penney would pop up in the number one spot.

I have never met a woman with more determination, perseverance and patience in my whole 34 years of practice life. This is indeed a woman who follows her heart, leans on the Lord, and in spite of life handing her some of the most overwhelming health problems and challenges that would fold almost anyone else, she continues to shine through it all. After all that, she keeps moving forward.

If you ever have the chance to meet her, you can feel the love of God emanating through her. You're not the same after making the acquaintance of Janet. She lifts up anyone that comes into her presence.

I originally met Janet years ago when she had pain in her body that medical science had been unable to pin down. She'd been inspected, prodded, poked, examined, invaded, probed, and tested with every imaginable device and test that could be ordered- all with no result. The symptoms were continually growing worse. A little time and treatment with me, and at least, we had a start on improvement. Her recovery, while not a complete 100%, was still a major victory. With that, she was back in the game of life and moving full speed ahead.

But life has a funny way of turning us down roads that we can never foresee coming. For Janet, it was a fall that shattered both wrists, then the lung cancer with surgery and treatment, just to name a couple of the big ones. We won't even talk about the emotional traumas of life, like losing her best friend to an early and untimely death.

In spite of it all, she didn't quit. She didn't quit making music for God. She didn't quit living her life. She didn't quit on anybody, including her family or herself.

It's been my blessing to have had her life cross my path, you know what, I'm a better and more keenly aware person to have had that blessing, there is no doubt. Enjoy her words that follow here, and the life lessons they share. They'll touch your heart and inspire your being. They will also lighten your journey. Knowing Janet has certainly done that for me."

Mabbett K. (Tad) Reckord III, D.C.
Family Chiropractic Health Center
Lakeland, Florida

"It has been my great honor to watch Janet move from a dark place to a place of joy as her courage and resilience have brought her into light. Her willingness to share her journey with such unvarnished candor is a testament to the healing power of a determined heart. It will inspire others to find their way back to the intended joy they deserve."

Joene Sussex
LCSW/CAP

"It was in the beginning months of my third internship that I attended my first AA meeting. I was nervous, naturally petrified, and a bit concerned how I would be received by the group. Besides, how would an inexperienced, student intern be viewed in a room full of alcoholics? Like everyone else present that morning, I was loved without hesitance and accepted without inquiry. No wonder the late Brennan Manning so accurately described AA as the spirit in which the church should aspire to. But aside from the recanting of the serenity prayer and free coffee, another sacred possession lies within the timeless candor of AA; the emphasis of holistic care and healing. This was best captured by one of the facilitators in that very meeting when he stated, "I think we're all spiritual beings just trying to figure out what it means to be human." As both an ordained minister and pastoral psychotherapist, I find such a relief in this complicated juncture of one's spirituality and their humanity.

While healthcare reform is destined to rewrite much of our medical realities, its greatest gift may very well be in the weaving of faith and health. For many, however, this merging is not a new language but one they have been speaking for some time. Janet Penney is certainly someone who speaks, writes, and lives out of this unique origin. Her story and the deepened introspect by which she tells it causes this to be such an imperative book. While every Barnes and Noble Bookstore you can find carries a wide array of self-help books and over-spiritualized journals, there is a vast shortage of worthy reads. Nowadays, if you can blog or tweet personal opinions, then there awaits for you a publisher to help with your first novel. In this work, Mrs. Penney salvages the richness and integrity of writing from the heart. In my line of work, I am most appreciative of those who can tell their story but leave me something to reference in a future conference or upcoming paper. Without the euphoria of a prosperity gospel or the coldness of a clinical note, Janet helps the reader connect the divine to the distorted. She doesn't shy away or seek refuge by running from one to the other. Rather, she carefully balances her walk with God with her walk through moments of sheer godlessness. I applaud her commitment to viewing the providence of

God, not as immunity from life's circumstances, but as God's unwavering presence with her.

So Janet, thank you for reminding me of 'the hope that lies within' our story and the One who keeps building on our story to tell. May the God of all life and love be with you my friend."

Rev. Will Eads,
MDiv-Clinical Resident

Preface

About midway through my time in Jerusalem, while gracefully allowing my friend Louann to groom me for the day, I made the comment, "I am going to write a book about all this and title it *Journey through Jerusalem*." She piped up and said, "With no hands!" "Yes," I quickly agreed. The Holy Spirit within me bore witness that I should record the events of going on such a journey with two broken wrists, and specifically to release the intricate details of my personal challenges. Illuminating how God in His faithfulness walked with me and brought miracle after miracle in my daily regime and beyond.

Unless you have been physically limited in such a way, you may find the details mundane. But then, wrap your mind around the words- *you can't do anything*. Imagine the moment by moment trust one would have to have for the simplest of tasks just within the privacy of their home, much less, to travel across the oceans to play the piano and sing over Jerusalem.

Within months of returning from Israel, the struggle for my life truly began after being diagnosed with a very aggressive lung cancer. All these things comprised, plummeted me into the most intense battle of all: the sanity of my own soul. I knew I had to be equipped or get whipped. I did not want to lose the beauty of God that was on my life due to the heat of my trials, yet I did not want the shine and glitter without substance.

> *"For no sooner has the sun risen with a burning heat*
> *then it withers the grass; its flower falls, and its beautiful*
> *appearance perishes"* (James 1:11a, NKJV).

God has traded me wealth for my warfare during these strategic periods of purpose. Discovering that any honorable destination in which we are privileged to arrive at, will not come without price, and will not end without great value. God grant you the ears to hear the sound of Heaven touching earth through the chorus of my testimony.

Acknowledgements

I would like to thank:

Martha Powell, my mother, for having long-distance conversations with me on the phone, listening to my stories written. You have given me great encouragement with your *tears of affirmation* each time I shared book portions; always giving me recall of things I had forgotten. Mama, you are a saint in my eyes; when I grow up, I want to be just like you. I love you dearly.

Barbara Jenkins, my only sister, thanks for always believing in me and filling my life with trinkets of treasures displaying your love. Thank you for listening, and for helping spread the testimonies of His Goodness. Your faith is an inspiration. I love you Sissy.

To Mitchell, my only son, a man after God. My love for you runs as deep and strong as the most rampant river. Thank you Bubba, for allowing the prophetic voice of God to speak through you, you have given me guidance more than you know. The world needs more of that, *I need more of that!*

To Charity, my oldest daughter, radiating your contagious zest for life; always showing honor to what God is doing in me… thank you, Char! You have grown into the most amazing godly wife and mother. The family values you walk out daily undeniably display the beautiful virtuous woman that you have become- Eternal love!

To my youngest daughter Leah, you have run alongside me with vision, while writing your own book. Thank you my princess, you are a jewel. I have called you my shadow since you were 6 years old, and now that you're 26, I want to shadow you! The purity and holiness you emanate is exactly what the whole world needs to follow. I will love you forever Lele!

To my six exuberant grandchildren, Eden-Glory, Gavin, Benjamin, Mitchell, Gabriel and Anna- you put the colors in my rainbow of life!

To my sweet husband Phillip, you put up with my whining woes, listened to my ecstatic joys, and always backed me in prayer throughout the process of writing this manuscript for the past several years. Thanks for never leaving me in my low estate, but always bringing me back up to par. You, my best friend, are amazing!

To Pastor Louann Moore who faithfully sojourned with me. Although it was never easy-*you* made it possible. Your daring faith has left an indelible mark on my life… I will forever love you with deep covenant love!

A special thanks to the small army of intercessors that God has placed around me: **Michele, Lynda, Sandra, Darlene, Kelly, Janice, Carmen, Carrie, Sylvia and Linda.** Any names exempt here-know that your prayers are not exempt from my heart and eternity. Thank you for standing your post and interceding for me.

To my staff-

Jamee, you spent tedious hours proofreading, and using your remarkable computer skills to bring alignment to my manuscript, including your selfless dedication in the submission process-without a doubt, you have been sent from God to be my friend, my true friend.

Kelly, you are my extra pair of eyes. This finished work would not have been possible without the days and days we spent together editing. Your faithful love and support has given me the necessary strength to go the duration of the project.

Lynda, you have a knack at always keeping me on task and truly carrying the vision. Your passion for Israel is a zealous fire that continuously burns bright and invigorates the call of God within me.

I could not have completed this project without you three amazing women. Because our paths divinely crossed, this work was made jovial- May God's abundant blessings be yours.

Jared Yates of JAREDESIGNS.COM for designing the cover of this book. You did a *spectacular* job conveying my hearts vision. Thanks a million!

A very special thanks to my partners who helped financially with this major undertaking and equipping me with the tools I needed… you know who you are.

I am eternally grateful to my Lord Jesus Christ who has graced me to pour out of my heart for the hope of reaching one soul. The One who has allowed me to walk up to the realms of glory, and down to the valley of the shadow of death and live to tell my story- so all who read can know; if he did it for me, he will do it for you.

Introduction

My Journey

As you read these pages, find yourself stepping into the streets of the City of the Great King with me. Within the three parts of my writings, let's journey together as I tell the unique story of what I encountered *on my way there, while I was there,* and *what happened after I left.*

As I walk in the season of embracing our Messiah's unending love, please to join me. Allow yourself to laugh and cry as you find me lost in the Judean Wilderness in the middle of the night. Let compassionate tears flow as I stand in the place where Jesus wept over Jerusalem, and experience a love above all loves for His chosen people. You might perceive a twinge of fear as an Israeli teenager is gunned down just outside the prayer room where we are praying. Hear my humbled heart beating as I play and psalm on a beautiful grand piano overlooking the City of David. Feel the depths of despair as I face traumatizing moments, along with the magnificent heights of His glory as His power sustains me. Feel the water splash on your face as I joyfully swim in the Sea of Galilee declaring His faithfulness. My aim is that these volumes paint a picture for you. Desiring not only to be the artist, but to be the paint stroking the vibrant colors from my heart upon the canvas of yours. Taste the passion of His mercy as I relinquish my very soul through bleak and hopeless days, as His amazing grace resounds.

Pleasantly permit the words to whet your appetite. Furthermore, increasing your own hearts capacity to experience a new dimension of intimacy with God. Sense the pulsating love that He has especially for you. Otherwise, the time spent composing this book will hold no eternal value. Behold the providence of our Lord as He wraps Himself around me and carries me on my journey through Jerusalem with no hands.

Prologue

Mandate

My ears perked up when I heard there was going to be a regional meeting to discuss the prayer movement that is currently sweeping the earth. Longing to increase awareness on this subject, I knew I had to attend. Concluding the teaching portion, the instructor of the class asked me to play the piano, sing and pray with the present team of intercessors. I was honored to be a part of the session. Afterwards, one of the attendees, that I did not know, picked up one of the House of Prayer brochures for my local church, and thought that she might join one of my prayer sessions in the future. Not knowing that a few years down the road, our paths would cross again in the telling of this life-changing story.

Previously in 2008, I bowed my knees at a world-wide prayer conference that was being held in Missouri. Here is where I had the most life changing encounter with God imaginable.

It was the last morning of the year and as I stood with over 20,000 people in attendance; the Holy Spirit began to draw people forward to consecrate their lives regarding a deeper commitment to prayer.

As He beckoned me with His love, I came to the front and knelt down with my face toward the floor. While sobbing uncontrollably, I sensed that I wanted to give my life forever to worship and intercessory prayer.

There on my knees, these words streamed out of my heart and mouth: *God, if I didn't work a public job, I would spend my days in prayer!* Wrenched to the very core, I knew I touched Heaven and Heaven touched me. When the services concluded on New Year's Eve, I packed my bags, and drove my rental car to the airport, waiting my return flight home to Lakeland, Florida. Back at work on January 2nd, my employer informed me that I was being laid off from my job. They were doing cutbacks and since I was the last one hired, I was being let go. The budget allowed me to work a few more weeks until my release. My heart was jolted to say the least, as I replayed over in my mind the prayer I uttered just two days before at the altar.

While at the prayer conference, I had received revelation of *Anna;* the prophetic intercessor in the Bible. She spent her life in prayer and fasting for sixty years in the Temple. I learned that the same anointing that Anna carried was returning upon the earth. It is being given to equip us for this end-time prayer movement, ultimately preparing us to become the spotless bride of Christ; concurrently bringing in the second coming of Jesus, our Bridegroom.

Anna's was the name of the store where I had been employed; it was beautifully designed with soft Christian music playing in the background. The entire store was permeated with the peace of God. In the two years I was privileged to work there it was part of my duty to greet each customer that walked through the door with these words, "Welcome to *Anna's!*" Those final weeks on my job, I began to hear with my spiritual ears these words instead: *Welcome to the house of the intercessor who prayed for sixty years!* What a declaration was being repeated for those several years that I worked there. It was as if I was speaking destiny into my own life with each greeting.

Now, here I am, leaving my public job knowing that God placed upon me a fresh mandate to stand in a place of night and day prayer. It seemed surreal, yet I realized by all this that I was becoming an end-time *Anna.* I recognized Heaven's thrust moving me into position. I began to pray and fast like never before, so much that I began to lose weight. Even though I was a born-again spirit-filled believer for over thirty years, I had not experienced such a burning desire to pray. Aching to give myself to God in a greater way, I went for more impartation at the *International House of Prayer* in Kansas City. This is where I saw God calling people from the far corners of the earth. I met people from Egypt, Turkey, Japan, and

Iceland. People hungry to be used by God during this final sweep across the earth; to call in the great harvest of souls before Jesus' return.

Shortly after engaging in such a rigorous lifestyle of prayer, I shared the vision of having a *house of prayer* within the walls of our church. My pastor acknowledged the mandate I had received from God, and sent me for additional, extensive, training and impartation in Kansas City. After my return, I was released to run with the vision and passion of my heart.

Two years later, with others catching the vision with me, and the prayer room running six days a week; I found myself completely lovesick for Jesus. Afforded by God this amazing privilege to stand in a place of leadership, to teach, and train others of a lifestyle of prayer, was rewarding. My total abandonment brought such a heavenly bliss. I knew, that I knew, that I knew, I was brought into the Kingdom for such a time as this.

Contents

Part 1

On My Way There

Chapter 1

~ *One Divine Invitation* ~

Sitting in a meeting with our Pastor this particular morning, one of the leaders turned to me and said, "Oh, by the way Janet, someone from Israel called the church office and asked for you today." Taken back by her words, I thought, *who in Israel knows me?* She gave me the information to return the call. I looked at my Pastor across the room and said, "What do I do?" The response was simple. "Call them."

You know it isn't every day that you get a phone call from Israel; it was a stunning yet pleasant surprise.

I made contact with a lady named Ruth* within a few days. She had called from the Jerusalem House of Prayer and she wanted to inform me that I had been selected as a delegate to represent the United States of America. I was invited to attend the fourteen-day All Nations Convocation for prayer leaders in the beautiful city of the Great King- Jerusalem.

> "But I say unto you, swear not at all; neither by heaven; for it is God's throne: for by the earth; for it is his footstool: neither by *Jerusalem; for it is the city of the great King*." (Matthew 15:34–35, KJV) *emphasis mine*

Her job was to contact at least one person from each nation to stand as an ambassador for their country. Over 195 nations had already responded, now she was calling on the United States. I had to ask her these prodigious questions: "Why are you calling me, and how did you even know that I was the director of our local church's house of prayer?" I mean, wouldn't you want to know?

She gladly informed me that she had a list of houses of prayer, *HOP*, from all across the globe. That in itself was amazing. As she was looking over the list for the United States, she noticed that the state of Florida had more HOP than any other state in the union; so naturally she wanted to pull from Florida. As she went down the list of prayer directors, she randomly picked Janet Penney of Lakeland, Florida. I use the word *randomly* with speculation. I was being selected to come and pray at the Jaffa Gate which, from Israel, is pointing toward the United States and Canada. The design being set from the Jerusalem House of Prayer, is to strategically place the nation's ambassador at the proper Gate for its effectiveness. A person has more spiritual authority to pray and proclaim for the place from which they are from. The *Jaffa Gate* is also known as, *Gate of the Friend*, a reference to Abraham, the friend of God, Isaiah 41:8. The redemptive purposes of the Jaffa Gate is that Jerusalem will see Yeshua as a tower of refuge and put their trust in the Mighty One of Israel. The redemptive gift of the United States is to bring forth repentance, reconciliation, revival and restoration in the nations. The American democracy is a forerunner of its kind. The United States is a sanctuary of refuge and is also called to help birth God's purposes for the church. To bring the Jewish people back to their biblical homeland and to reveal the Messiah, Jesus Christ, to all who land on her shores.

The *Jerusalem House of Prayer* operates in the scriptural pattern of the *Tabernacle of David* in the Old Testament; to have worship and intercession flowing together in unison. I will elaborate on the Jerusalem House of Prayer in a latter chapter.

"And in mercy shall the throne be established; and he shall sit upon it in truth in the tabernacle of David, judging, and seeking judgment, and hasting righteousness." (Isaiah 16:5, kjv)

Many of the HOP flow in what is commonly called *Harp and Bowl* which stems from the book of Revelation.

I realized I had been doing this for decades in my own secret place with God, yet, I did not have the fullness of this revelation until recently. Praying and singing the scriptures have been a long-standing passion of mine.

My pastor soon released me to begin a ten-week training class on Wednesday nights on the subject of intercession. My cup was running over with joy in each session. As the house of prayer developed and grew, so did I. Queen Esther, as a young girl, who through a lifestyle of prayer and fasting, changed a nation and saved her Jewish people. Esther was a type and shadow of the end-time church. The body of Christ should be so devoted in a consecrated lifestyle of prayer that they change the world around them. Being given this opportunity to pray at the Jaffa Gate on behalf of my nation, I knew, could also bring great spiritual results. I was honored at being invited to be a small part of the equation.

Shortly after the establishment of my local church's house of prayer, I penned this spiritual song, according to the book of Esther.

"I was born for this moment, I was born for this
moment for such a time, such a time as this.
I was brought into the kingdom, I was brought into the
kingdom, for such a time, such a time as this.

When timing met destiny, when timing met destiny,
Esther set her people free, Esther set her people free."

We are called to be a part of setting people free through the intercession that we give, and by walking in the timing of the Lord.

> **"Speaking to yourselves in psalms and hymns and spiritual songs, singing and making melody in your heart unto the Lord." (Ephesians 5:19, KJV)**

Notice the verse says, "Singing and making melody…" This is what I would do repeatedly to affect the atmosphere around me and the movements of my own heart. God has been building *me* into a house of prayer; a structure that can never be moved by human hands.

Now unsure of what to do with this astounding invitation to Jerusalem; I gave my concern to my pastor. "Let's pray about it for a few days and see what God wants," was the reply.

On Friday of that same week, the person who had taken the brochure from the regional meeting had joined in at my church's house of prayer for the first time. The intercessors were specifically praying concerning the invitation that had been given me to go to Israel. I was told later, by her, that upon awakening that morning, she was *pressed* in her spirit to quickly dress and head out to locate our house of prayer. The urgency to go and join in with the intercessors was imperative. Yet, with the shyness of her nature, if she been had been late and the meeting had already started, she would have been hesitant to even walk in. Submitting to the Holy Spirit's prompting, she moved with great speed to be there on time. Isn't it amazing how the Spirit of God moves upon the hearts of men?

> **"And** *he came by the Spirit into the temple:* **and when the parents brought him the child Jesus, to do for him after the custom of the law, then took he him up in his arms and blessed God, and said, Lord let now thy servant depart in peace, according to thy word: for mine eyes have seen they salvation." (Luke 2:27–30, KJV)** *emphasis mine*

It is so important we respond swiftly to the Holy Spirit. We see in the above verse that Simeon could have missed his moment of destiny. How many times have we missed a very important moment that God had for us, simply because we procrastinated? Remember, delayed obedience, is disobedience. It can cost not only us, but other people who are involved. Further in the same chapter we see the prophetess Anna, also was compelled to come to the temple to be at Jesus' presentation.

> "And she was a widow of about fourscore and four years, which departed not from the temple, but served God with fastings and prayers night and day. And she coming in that instant…" (Luke 2:37–38a, KJV)

Simeon and Anna were both a vital part of what was happening at the baby dedication of Jesus. Notice the scripture says, *coming in that instant.* No delay could be afforded. Anna had literally been praying into fruition the first coming of the Lord for sixty years, and now she was privileged to see the fulfillment of her prayers. Imagine this moment for her.

Doesn't this put a desire inside you to pray, hear, and obey? Most times not even knowing the outcome, but just trusting God that He knows best and He has purpose in every single thing we do; that alone should inspire us to pray.

As this person, who was being led by the Holy Spirit to my churches house of prayer, made her way into the room, she met the team of intercessors. They all made her feel welcomed, adjacent with the sweet presence of Jesus. As the director, I had appointed leaders for each prayer session which instructed the team with what the prayers needs were. Also, each person had an assigned time of prayer, so I was not present on this specific day.

As they concluded with the two-hour prayer set, she left as quickly as she came. **Being urgently compelled again by the Holy Spirit** to drive home and get her check book and return to pay the $3,000 that I needed to go to Israel. She stated, "If anybody needs to represent the United States of America, it would be Janet Penney." Earlier, at the regional meeting, her heart had recognized the gift of intercession in me and graciously appreciated it. When all this transpired, Louann, who was appointed to lead the house of prayer that day, yelled out at the top of her voice, "I'm going too! If He did it for you, He'll do it for me! I'm going, if I have to carry your bags, I'm going with you!"

Needless to say, she was very inspired by what had just taken place. Wouldn't you be? I did not even know this precious saint, yet she adamantly obeyed God and wrote a $3,000 check for my trip in one instant of time. My Pastor called me later that day and said, "Janet, I am holding a check here in the office for you; it looks like God wants you in Jerusalem." Together, we acknowledged that the timing of the Lord is a perfect thing indeed. As I hung up the phone and lay across my bed and began to sob, "This is so big God, I am humbled that *You* are calling *me* to Israel, and You have divinely paid the way." I trembled as I lay there scarcely able to take it all in. It seemed as if God had kissed my life that delightful day.

In our 3-D world of width, breadth, and height, we sometimes skim over what Einstein calls the fourth dimension. A thing called *time*. Scientist defines it as a measurement, a dimension, the time space continuum.

Webster's Dictionary terms it this way: *an appointed moment or hour for something to happen.*

As a believer, I know that time is a space in eternity where human activity meets up with an earthy process.

"**Is there anything too hard for the Lord? At** *the appointed time* **I will return unto thee, according to the time of life, and Sarah shall have a son.**" **(Genesis 18:14, KJV)** *emphasis mine*

Baby Isaac, was in the heart of God waiting for the intimate, human activity of his parents to complete the earthly process of actually bearing the child. The relativity of time and space, a necessary component of which my heart prefers to call: destiny.

Such detailed dimensions of God are worthy of searching out.

Breadth (n)-something of full width, a comprehensive quality.

Length (n)-the longest dimension, a distance or extent in space, duration of time.

Depth(n)-the condition of being tall or high, the quality of being deep, a degree of intensity, quality of being profound, complete or thorough.

Height (n)-the most advanced point, summit, and Zenith.

Do you not agree that these are excellent descriptions of Jehovah's great love?

He is my all in all, my exceeding joy. There is none higher or deeper in volume. Truly there is no God like our God. My heart resonates this song that I recently wrote.

Elohim Adonia, my God, my life
My Savior my Lord, Jesus Christ
Jehovah Shammah, the Lord present, Jehovah Rapha, the
Lord my healer Jehovah Jireh, He provides my needs
Jehovah Nissi, my banner lifted high. Jehovah Shalom my peace
El-elyon, the Most High
El Shaddai, God of the mountain, the mothering kind
Abba, Advocate, Almighty, the Amen
Ancient of Days, the Beginning and the End
Anointed One, Author, finisher of my faith
Branch that I grow from. The Countenance on my face
Bread of God, Breathe of Life, breathing in me

Bright and Morning Star, Chief Shepherd, Comforter,
Commander, Counselor, Creator and King
Deliverer, Door, Desire of all Nations
Eternal One, Faithful Witness, Firstborn
among many brethren, my Foundation
Great High Priest
Good Shepherd, the Bleating of the Sheep
Head of the Church, Holy One of Israel, Horn of my Salvation
Lover of my soul, my firm Foundation
Image of God, Immanuel, God with us, Jealous Lover and Judge
You are JESUS-my Hightower, in You I put my trust
King of Kings, King of the Ages
Lamb slain from the foundation
Law Giver, Leader, Life, Lily of the Valley, Lion of the Tribe of Judah,
descending like a dove
Corner Stone, Living Stone, Living Water, Lord of Glory,
Lord of Hosts, Lord of Lords, Pure Sweet Love
Man of Sorrows, acquainted with grief
Mediator, Master, Merciful, Messenger,
Messiah, You are the Nazarene
Offspring of David, Only Begotten Son
You are the Only One... the Only One...
found worthy to open the seals.
Potter, Prophet, Purifier
Redeemer, Rock, Refiner's Fire
Yes Refiner's Fire and Fullers Soap
Great Physician making me whole
Resurrection, Root of David
Rose of Sharon, Ruler of Creation
Savior, Seed, Servant and Shield, Son of
David, Son of God, Son of Man
Teacher, Truth, You are the Great I Am
The Vine that I cling to, All Wisdom, the Truth, the Life, the Way

The Wheel in the Middle of the Wheel, the
Trinity, Holy Ghost, Father and Son
Amazing, Eternal, The Godhead Three in One
The Word of God made Flesh
It's *You* Jesus- the One I love unto the death

**"His eyes were as a flame of fire and on His head were
many crowns and** *He had a name written that no man knew
but He Himself."* **(Revelation 19:12, KJV)** *emphasis mine*

Imagine this; He has a Name that has never been heard, voiced, or penned! My mind cannot fathom a Name sweeter than Jesus. He is an amazing God and is forever transforming us. There is no way to really measure Him. Our God is Omnipotent and Omnipresent, Alpha and Omega, the Beginning and the End. In my frail attempt to describe Him, I fail, because He is so much more than these mere human words. So why would I not want to totally abandon myself unto Him, when He is so profound and thorough with each detail of my life? I find as I lean into Him and allow His Spirit to capture me, the more I actually do comprehend His vast love.

**My heart is indicting a good matter: I speak of the things
which I have made concerning the King: my tongue
is the pen of a ready writer."** **(Psalms 45:1, KJV)**

Having a *tongue as the pen of a ready writer* is in modern terms being a *skilled writer*. This gift must be honed. Open your mouth and let His praise not only be in your heart, but on your tongue, speaking forth His glorious majesty. Begin to stretch your vocabulary with greater volumes and dimensions during your worship time. As you do, in return, God will begin to increase your capacity for more of Who He really is. In actual fact, the previous song came to me through a desire that I had for a greater expression during my personal worship time, leading me into a study on the Names of God. He longs to have Himself etched on your heart and mind. Which will better able you to share Him with others.

If you become a writer or not, it will help you to exemplify a life that leads people around you into a closer walk with the One True God. Ask Him to invade your *space* and your *time*, and you may just find yourself standing in places you never dreamed possible.

---

* Due to the sensitive nature of the ministry, the name has been changed.

Chapter 2

~ *The Accident* ~

"My wrists are broken! My wrists are broken!" I screamed among the crowd while questioning in my own mind what my eyes were beholding. "My wrists are broken and I have to go to Israel and play the piano!" Anger, fear, disbelief, all encumbered me as I lay on the floor underneath a woman who had fallen on top of me.

The praise was high and the worship was deep that night in our revival service. The guest speaker had petitioned us all forward at the climax of the service. Well over 200 people were surrounding the altar as the fire of God enveloped us. My hands were raised and my eyes closed as I was savoring His sweet aroma. Then in an instant, I was literally slammed to the floor, seemingly knocked unconscious for a brief moment. An onlooker stated that it looked as if a car had hit me because I was struck with such great velocity. In half a second, my whole world was altered.

Now somehow, in a seated position on the floor, my eyes looked down to where I was feeling a strange numbness. What I saw took my breath away; grotesquely my hands had swollen as the bones in my wrists were practically protruding out. My arms and hands were horribly misshapen. All I could think of was the trip to Israel that I was to take in less than three weeks; that's when my ear piercing screams started.

"My wrists are broken and I have to play the piano!" I yelled to my friend Louann as she knelt down toward me. "Get up" she said, not realizing what had happened. Then her eyes saw my mangled hands and arms. It was then she tugged on the pastor's shoulder. In a matter of moments, I was lifted very gently from the sanctuary altar and carefully placed on the sofa in the pastor's office. While my pastor was on bended knees, face to face with me, began wiping my forehead with a cool wet cloth.

I vaguely heard someone say that the paramedics were on their way. My mind was whirling with confusion, every face I saw and each voice I heard seemed indistinct. Where was I? Who was I? What happened to me?

Surrounding by the church leadership, they were all encouraging me not to look at my hands; which by now were swollen twice their normal size. Instead of fear, words of faith began to rise from them all. Please learn the dynamic of this faith principle. We cannot be moved by what we *see*, we must only be moved by what we *believe*.

The pastor's words were - **"Janet, you will go to Israel, you <u>will</u> go to Israel. If we have to hire a private nurse to travel with you, you <u>will</u> go."**

Those words were like a warm, smooth dagger going deep within my being. You would think at such a moment of crisis, that there would not be so much faith for my imminent journey, but there was. I believe this trip was such a part of my destiny that it could not be negated even due to this traumatic turn.

Now here I am being fit on a gurney headed toward the hospital. Earlier that day I had met with the pastor and the core leadership team of intercessors in that very room, *on that very couch!* I had shared with them how through my study of Israel, I discovered that the Sea of Galilee was the shape of a harp. It is told that as the wind blows, you can hear the cords of the harp wisping across the water for miles around. Ecstatic, my heart leapt within me! How inviting that sounded… I *had* to swim in the Sea of Galilee! The piano, which is the modern day harp, had been the love of my life for over thirty years. My desire intensified daily at just the possibility that I could actually swim there and satisfy my heart.

As the transporters began to roll me into the ambulance, my pastor said to me, **"You will swim in the Sea of Galilee!"** Glancing at my broken limbs, you can only imagine the doubt that tried to enshroud me.

Right then and there I had a decision to make; to walk in faith or to be moved by what I saw. The choice was there, yet because I was hemmed in by strong truth-bearing people, their un-staggering faith imparted into me the strength and forbearance I needed to believe the impossible.

My husband Phillip was standing outside the door of the ambulance as it swung open; his eyes were filled with fear of the unknown. He was at work when he received the call that I had been injured and was on the way to the emergency room. Inside the small partitioned hospital room, as the commotion settled down, the pain began to escalate. The initial shock was wearing off and words cannot describe the anguish I was now experiencing. During the delicate removal of the paramedics bubble wrap braces, all eyes in the room were on the injured site. Looking at what used to be my small thin arms, hands and fingers, which were now severely swollen and distorted, Phillip had to turn away so I would not see the pain and fear on his face. He had listened to years and years of me playing joyfully on my piano. He was thinking of my passionate love for it, and knew, more than anyone, that playing was a major part of my expression to God.

We both cried as the doctor explained that both wrists had received bilateral compound fractures and that surgery was absolutely necessary. They had been shattered completely in half, leaving them only to dangle uselessly at the end of my arms. Each wrist would have permanent titanium metal plates and screws placed inside them. The doctor said he would have to put the metal plates across the entire wrist preventing any flexibility or movement.

Here again the choice tried to present itself: to believe or to doubt. Have you ever been there? Think about it, has life thrown you an unexpected curve ball? Thinking, "Oh God what is going on! This is not the way things are supposed to be!" Sure, all of us have experienced the doubts and fears of hard, unexpected times; yet learning to handle things optimistically carries us through such trials of devastation.

As I was being wheeled into surgery, Phillip asked the doctor, "Realistically, will she be able to use her hands without too much debilitation? I want to know because she plays the piano every day?"

Quickly whisking me away behind those frightening operating room doors the doctor said, "She may never play the piano as before."

Ouch! How the words violated everything within me. Like a volcanic eruption these words spewed forth from my lips; *"I will play better!"*

Chapter 3

~ *One-Two-Two and a Half-Three* ~

—◦◦◦◦◦◦◦◦—

I am sure many of you have had experiences when you were presented with this thing called *choice*. Maybe obstacles loomed over you just waiting for you to recede. It may have been a life or death situation or maybe something not so drastic. Which job should I take? Should I move out of state? Who am I supposed to marry? Which school should my child attend? Choices, choices, choices are awaiting us every single day. Our goal is to learn the art of letting our own hearts choose; to be led by our spirit not our soul. God wants His people to be proficient at following His lead, knowing His voice at all times and to obey quickly. To call those things that be not as though they were.

> **"(As it is written, I have made thee a father of many nation,) before him who believed, even God, who quickeneth the dead, and calleth those things which be not as though they were." (Romans 4:17, KJV)**

That's what I was doing. I was declaring that day on my way to the operating table, that I would play the piano better *after* the restraining metal plates were permanently installed in my arms than I did *before*.

When we take the middle ground in our lives, when we know better, and most times we *do* know better, unfortunately we end up eating the fruit of those choices.

I like to say it this way; when we tell our young children to do a particular thing and they run and play to purposefully ignore us, we adapt to their little game playing and say "You'd better do it or I'll count to three." Then we teasingly laugh and say very slowly, *one... two... two and a half... three.* We stretch it out as long as we can then the child scurries to obey. Unfortunately we treat our Heavenly Father the same way. Procrastinating in our obedience is always a wrong choice. It is not healthy to negotiate with God or try to bargain our way through something, He longs for a trusting heart and faithful relationship. To our ill fate, we pay the consequences of bad timing along with bad judgment when both could have been avoided with doing the right thing at the right time. Simply heeding the words of the Lord quickly, should be our appropriate response.

I recall when my oldest daughter, Charity, was about two and a half years old. We were in our front yard, attending to a garage sale when I told her to stay close to me and she slipped away without my notice. Within a few moments, I had a prompting of impending danger. My eyes began to look to and fro, no Charity anywhere. I was frantic! I searched around the tables nearest the road and there she was just sitting on the curb watching the cars go by. Had I waited a minute longer, it may have turned out badly. In case you did not know, most two-year olds do not stay sitting for very long. Later that day, I chuckled at the trusting thought of her angel standing in front of her with his hand pressing on her forehead saying, "Don't you move until your Mommy gets here." In our innocence of ignorance, or reasoning rebellion, our untimely games can be very costly.

Graciously, Louann told me after surgery, that God had spoken to her to stand in front of me just moments before the accident; which would have positioned her to break the fall of the person who fell. As she pondered the thought, *bam*, I was on the floor underneath the other person.

We live in a real world which implicates we are not invincible, just human flesh and bones.

Could this incident have been avoided? Could many things we encounter have been avoided? The bankruptcy? The divorce? The unwanted pregnancy? Choices ultimately make us into the person we need to become, or break us into many scattered pieces not knowing where we belong. May our hearts be so developed to the point where Our Father does not have to play the 1-2-3 game with us? In our moments of delay, we typically end up paying the price we did not want to pay. It is in the doubt, fear, and compromise of our own soul where the balance is weighed. Should I go, or should I stay? Should I sleep, or should I pray? Should I do this tomorrow, or should I do this today? There is an endless array of choices. I have learned that even when I do not understand, I still choose Him.

Like I said earlier, I am grateful my friend shared with me the delay of her heart obedience. She did not have to, but she did. It spoke volumes to both of us that day, and we learned a valuable lesson that we all can glean from.

> **"For I the Lord thy God will hold thy right hand, saying unto thee, Fear not; I will help thee." (Isaiah 41:13, KJV)**

Let that sink in a little; *God holds your hand.* That would depict He is walking with you, no matter how difficult the path your life is on, He knows all and sees all. He longs for you to choose Him and follow His lead, and by choosing Him, you choose life; in doing so, you will bring Him great delight.

> **"And Samuel said, hath the Lord as great delight in burnt offerings and sacrifice as in obeying the voice of the Lord? Behold to obey is better than sacrifice and to hearken than the fat of rams." (1 Samuel 15:22, KJV)**

"Help us Father to live a life syncopated with Heaven's rhythm; every time Father *You* exhale, let *us* inhale your instructions, and speedily follow it out."

My daughter-in-law started telling my firstborn granddaughter, when she was a toddler, to make good choices. I think we should adapt this simple phrase into our vocabulary and our lifestyle.

Did you know it only takes seven seconds for your brain to analyze a person, place, or thing? Within seven seconds after a person approaches you, you can detect if that person is friend or foe, trustworthy or deceitful, if this is a person you want to avoid or embrace. At lightning speed, we make a choice. In seven seconds first impressions are made that last forever. You can never undo a first impression. Some choices are irreversible as well. So, if the human brain has such a capability, think about when you are faced with a gamut of choices that will affect your destiny. You are the master of your decisions, but you become a slave to your choices.

So at the end of the day, or should I say, at the end of life, you will have become what you have chosen.

> "I call heaven and earth as witnesses today against you, that
> I have set before you life and death, blessing and cursing;
> therefore *choose life*, that both you and your descendants
> may live." (Deuteronomy 30:19, NKJV) *emphasis mine*

Chapter 4

~ *Israel or Bust* ~

At the departure time of my seven day hospital stay, the nurse was wheeling me to the front door; I glanced over in the lobby area and noticed a lovely black grand piano. My heart was being drawn to it, so I asked to be wheeled over beside this magnificent instrument. In the wounds of my bruised and bleeding soul, I wondered if I would truly be able to live out my passion again for the enemy seemed to attack the very essence of who I was.

I asked Phillip, my husband, to lift the cover as I daringly placed one very weak finger on the ivories.

As the pain seared through my arms and hands I pressed one key and exclaimed, "I cannot be contained!" This one key, this one note, this one sound, started me on my road to freedom.

I knew I had to decree and declare that I would not succumb to the words of the doctor that said *I would not play as before*. My mouth had to proclaim the victory I knew lay ahead for me. I knew there must be a demand placed upon my faith which expelled that *I would not be contained or confined within walls of disability*. This would be key to my survival.

Arriving home that day, to my surprise, there was a hospital bed beside the large window in our family room. My sweet husband knew I could not manage comfortably in our bed. You see, to reduce the swelling of my hands, I had to keep them pointed upward at all times, even in my sleep. He tenderly propped my arms with pillows as I lay in an elevated position. This is where I remained until I left to board the airplane destined for Israel. Phillip is an amazing man of God, full of compassion, he hurts when I hurt. God has given me my soul-mate who carries me on the wind of his prayers and the simplicity of his servant's heart.

Over the next few weeks, many guests came by to visit me. Some were skeptical about my eminent trip, while others were inspired that I would even dare to still go. But how could I *not* go when the invitation seemed so divine and all expenses were miraculously paid? Everything seemed to be in order, well almost everything. My soul had its own doubts naturally. In my human frailty, I sometimes wanted everyone to go away and leave me in my broken condition. In reality, I could not even flip a light switch, much less play the piano. I recall a friend from church; she came by and provoked me to exercise my weak fingers. She insisted that I placed each one on the tip of my thumb and count to 195, to represent each of the 195 nations that would be represented in Jerusalem. This was so challenging.

From elbows to fingertips, I was completely braced and I had not used my fingers at all for well over a week now. It was a bit strenuous, but I tried to appease her to do this seemingly small task. After my friend left that day, I continued exercising my hands and fingers in my private time, and I began to pray for the nations and my upcoming journey. Not only did my hands begin to gain strength, so did my soul. Somehow I knew I would be able to go the distance no matter the paramount obstacles in my way. My heart was beginning to beat for what lie ahead for me in Israel. Sure I had my apprehensions because of two broken wrists and all that was involved, yet, deep within I knew it was a moment of destiny for me.

My daughter, Charity, came to care for me one day during the first week of my rehabilitation. Along with her was her four-year-old son. His eyes were big with anticipation when he saw the neat hospital bed that his Grandma was in. He was eager to sit on the bed with me. Being intrigued with the remote attached to the side of the bed, he asked if he could push the buttons. Thinking it would be harmless, and could even bring some fun to my day, I let him. As the two of us went up and down we laughed and giggled. On the final descent of the bed, he begged to go up just one more time. With him being my firstborn grandson, and looking into his adorable little face; how could I deny him? To this day I wish I had. Unfortunately, as the bed began to lower, it somehow came detached from its frame, and me, Gavin, and the bed tipped over and came tumbling down. With all my weight and his, we both landed on my left arm as I began to scream in agony. Trauma on top of trauma, pain on top of pain! My sweet little grandson was so frightened at the sound of my cry, that he started crying along with me.

As my family helped me up, the anger I felt from reinjuring myself overwhelmed me. I was not angry with Gavin. No, instead of putting *him* in his place, I put *myself* in his place. He was sad that he had allowed me to get hurt. It was not his fault at all; the bed was the faulty one. I gave him a gentle hug as I walked up the steps toward my bedroom. I had not spent any time in my own room since the accident. The only world I knew was in the family room. Closing the door behind me with my foot, I somehow crawled up into the middle of my bed and wept bitterly. My mind kept thinking of the healing process that would now be prolonged for my left wrist. A few minutes later my husband came in to check on me. What spewed from my mouth that day surprised him and more inescapably startled me.

"Leave me alone and don't bother me, I do not want any visitors; I do not want any phone calls, turn off the light, shut the door and go away!"

I lay in my dark room the rest of the day and on into the night feeling so discouraged. Some may have called it a pity party, but it felt so much more than that to me. Phillip came to the door to feed me, I declined and he gently backed out of the room and left me completely alone. Have you ever been feeling low and the enemy gave you another kick to push you even lower? Sometimes you think that you cannot take one more thing, inevitably you do. You grab hold of His grace and try to climb back up.

By morning, I was still lying there with pillows propping up my hands. In my forlorn state, the door quickly swung open and in bolted

Louann; flipping on the light. I screamed, "Turn that light off!" As she turned it off, she said, "How can I read the Bible devotional to you in the dark?" I gave her no response. She sat down on the floor next to a small lamp and asked if she could turn that on instead. When I hesitantly looked at her, she was beaming, I mean smiling from ear to ear! She said, "Guess what?" Still I gave no response. I did not want her or anyone in my bedroom, especially someone so cheerful. She began to blurt out words so fast I could not even understand her. After all, I was medicated and had tuned out everyone and everything. Again, Louann tried to tell me that she was going to Jerusalem with me. She and our pastor had talked and agreed that I should not, and could not travel alone. Considering that Louann is a Certified Nurse's Assistant, it would be a good fit. But the final decision for her to attend would be up to me.

Inconsolably, I said, "You go to Jerusalem, I'm not going!" as I turned my face to the wall.

It was a good thing she was so charged with excitement. The faith that was emerging out of her heart and mouth compelled me to get up, leave that dark bedroom, and come out into the light of the family room. She put on some worship music that she knew I loved and walked out of the room. After marinating all night in disappointment, my heart now began to soak in the sounds of heaven that were filling the room. I closed my eyes and took inventory of the last twenty-four hours. This was so unlike me; I cannot recall experiencing such despondency. After about half an hour had passed, I recognized His love moving across my soul. Gentle tears flowed freely as I embraced again the call to Jerusalem. I could not let what happened victimize me; instead I must allow it to propel me into destiny.

Chapter 5

~ *Ice* ~

With just two days left before leaving for Israel, I went to the doctor to have the staples removed from my wrists. As he un-wrapped the surgery bandages, I wiggled around uncomfortably trying to cooperate with the nurse. No one had touched my hands or arms since the surgery so they were very tender, weak, and somewhat painful. After the first metal staple was removed, I winced with pain as a warm tear leaked from the corner of my eye. Looking down I noticed thirteen more staples that had to come out and then fourteen more on the other arm. "Oh no!" I bellowed. Louann piped up and said, "Sing Janet, sing!" Why in the world would I want to sing? I was too busy sobbing. She knew that singing would not only distract me, but it would lift my spirit as well and help charge my faith. The song, *I believe You're my Healer, I believe You're more than enough for me*, came quickly out of my mouth. Let me encourage you sing to the Lord in your time of pain, it honestly helps. He is Jehovah Rapha, the Lord your Healer.

The doctor proceeded to tell me about the cast he was going to apply, etc., and that after one full year my wrist would be as good as they were going to get. "One full year!" I exclaimed. "Yes, for the most part, but after a year the healing process would slow down and you should reach the maximum usage of your hands by the following year." The doctor stated. Two years of difficulty was not what I wanted to hear, yet I knew the bones and the metal had to collaborate. It was then I told him of my trip to Israel and that I was leaving the very next day. Gleefully, I told the doctor how I just *had* to swim in the Sea of Galilee, and that I could not decline the invitation to play the piano in Jerusalem. He was going to put me in two hard casts, then, he paused for a moment and said that he thought surgery strips and a Velcro brace would be sufficient. Hallelujah! If he had put both my arms in a hard cast, I could not get them wet in the shower much less the Sea of Galilee!

Early the next morning I literally climbed out of my hospital bed, while Louann and her husband Roger, plus Phillip, loaded the van heading toward the Orlando International Airport. I was edgy and tense being around the crowds of people there. The thought of someone bumping into me and bringing any additional pain was relentless. Louann was handling all her luggage and mine, and the tickets with our identification cards. She was a real trooper to be willing to undergo such an adventure with having to be four-handed instead of two. Fortunately, she had traveled overseas many times and knew the drill and hard work it took to endure.

With my arms and hands wrapped in braces, it was impossible to do anything. Can you wrap your mind around the words **can't do anything?** Tie your hands around your back for one day and you will get the picture.

Even with the modest duty of going to the restroom, someone had to accompany me; I mean every single time. Did I say that this process is particularly humbling? Now, imagine me about to board a plane to Israel and I can't even go to the restroom alone. I called my Mother/ prayer partner, and asked her to believe the best with me about this complication. Because you see, I was to be in the air for about sixteen hours and airplane restrooms are very tiny; two people could in no way fit. I am just being real with you my friend.

"The fear of the Lord is the instruction of wisdom; and before honor is humility." (Proverbs 15:33, KJV)

This was only *one* of the daily challenges I was facing. There was a great demand placed on my faith concerning this matter. When we face disability, He brings a-b-i-l-i-t-y.

At the airport, we were believing for what you might call a small miracle, but to me it was a huge miracle. On purpose, I wore a very loose dress that would be easy to deal with in the restroom; I could in no way unhook a button or use a zipper. I went to the ladies restroom alone for the first time since the accident. I walked by faith not by sight or feeling. Glory to God, He graced me to attend to myself. I came walking out of the restroom, smiled at Louann and said, "Let's go to Israel."

It is these tiny, baby steps of faith that pleases God so much. Do what you have to do and He will always meet you there. I got my huge miracle within minutes, just minutes, before boarding! I once heard a preacher say that the word *hurry* is not in God's vocabulary. I believe it! We may think he is slow or even late but in actual fact He is always right on time.

As we were seated on the front row of the aircraft, Louann opened her backpack and pulled out two large empty freezer bags. I thought, *what in the world?* When the flight attendant came our way, Louann kindly asked her if she could fill the bags up with ice. She smiled, nodded her head, and took the bags. Within minutes, she returned with the bags filled with ice. Louann began to take the braces off. Then, gently taking my arms, she placed them on top of the bags and said, "I don't want your hands to swell due to the air compression of the cabin, I think it could affect them." I sat there thinking, *Wow, she thinks of everything, how considerate is this? Maybe this journey without the use of my hands is going to work after all.*

Our words and actions are simply a reflection of what is in our hearts. My eyes were being opened to the humble servanthood of Jesus that was in the heart of this woman that God had ordained to accompany me.

We were now on our ascent into Jerusalem. If you know anything about the City of the Great King, you know that going there is always referred to *up*. Up, to Mt. Zion, up to the hill of the Lord. No matter where you are in the earth, Jerusalem is always up. Now my spirit began to lift *up* as well. Drenched with gratefulness, I could not, and did not want to stop the free flowing tears. Such joy was transcending down with the thought of going *up* to Jerusalem.

**"Pay attention to what you weep over, for your tears
will point you toward your destiny." Lou Engle**

I was breathing in the moment and thought, *What if we treasured
every single breath that God affords us? Wouldn't we be better off? Teach us
to breathe the breath of eternal life oh Lord.*

Flying over the Mediterranean Sea, I begin to sing a prophetic song
over Israel:

"Fire in your eyes and healing in your wings,
Son of God, Son of man speak to us we are listening.
Here we are your daughters, waiting for the voice of many waters."
We are not going to miss one moment of one hour of
one day of Your divine destiny. We are going to hear,
we are going to know, we're going to flow.
We are going to walk the streets of destiny.
We are going to fulfill everything you have placed on the inside of us.
I am going to walk, I am going to sing, I am going to prophesy,
I am going to speak new life through my lips of clay.
We are vessels prepared and ready to speak to set nations free.
With fire in Your eyes and healing in Your wings, come,
Jesus come, as we enter the streets of Jerusalem. Jerusalem
is calling my name; it will never be the same.
Get ready for the change in Jesus Name. Thank you Lord for taking us
where we are going, and thank you for taking us where we have been."

I lay my head back and rested in the Shalom of God for the first real
time since this journey started. Life is a gift, time is a gift, and friends are
a gift. Never take for granted what you have been given in this life. No
matter how rough the road; God can make the crooked places straight
for you because of His magnificent undying love. God does not just *have*
love, He *is* love. Jehovah Shammah, the Lord Is Present, is with you
on the airplane, in the operating room, the unemployment line or the
nursing home. No matter what is happening, big or small, He is with
you to strengthen you and give you peace.

> "The Lord will give strength unto His people; the Lord will bless His people with peace." (Psalm 29:11, KJV)

Let go of the disappointments that may haunt you. Start embracing the moment you are in right now; cling to the present, and dream of the good things that your Heavenly Father wants to do in your future. He will send help, and He will not forget you in your low estate. Even if you need a bag of ice to reduce the swelling of your body or soul, Jesus will provide.

Part 2

While I Was There

Chapter 6

~ *Humble Ambassador* ~

Humble (adj)-Ranking low; insignificant; expression offered in a spirit of submission.

Ambassador (n)-An authorized representative or messenger traveling abroad.

On my face one day in prayer, soon after I had been selected as a delegate to travel to Israel; I was pouring my heart out to the Lord, praying a difficult, yet earnest prayer. I said words that most people would not dare say to Him. I said "God, strip me of all my pride." I said those words because, going to Israel or not, I wanted a pure heart more than anything else and I say this with most sincerity. Sitting in the position of the house of prayer director, teaching, training, and leading others to the throne room, I must have purity flowing in and out of my vessel; anything less would be bring a tainted flow. I could not bear the thought of impurities filtering through my life and those same impurities affecting the lives of those entrusted to me. The cleaner a pipe is, the cleaner the water which flows from the pipe. This is how I view my heart.

> **"All have sinned and fallen short of the glory of God." (Romans 3:23, kjv)**

As humans, we do sin. The Bible declares in James 4:17 that if we know to do good, and don't do it, it is sin. Yet we can experienced the cleansing power of the blood of Jesus, and through that power, walk in purity. My greatest ambition has always been to walk daily in the holiness of Jesus.

> "And declared to be the son of God with power,
> according to the spirit of holiness, by the resurrection
> from the dead." (Romans 1:4, KJV)

I have been on that quest for over thirty-five years and am still on it. On this quest, I will remain until He changes me from mortality to immortality.

> "For we that are in this tabernacle do groan, being burdened: not
> for that we would be unclothed, but clothed upon, that mortality
> might be swallowed up of life." (2 Corinthians 5:4, KJV)

Within twenty-four hours of asking God to strip me of all my pride is when I found myself on the floor with two shattered wrists. Please hear me; I am *not* saying that God broke my wrists to teach me humility, but He sure used what the devil meant for evil, for my good and the good of many others.

> "You planned to harm me. But God planned it for
> good. He planned to do what is now being done. He
> wanted to save many lives." (Genesis 50:20, NIRV)

Certainly God is watching over us. He will use our testimonies to save the lives of others. He is good at being involved in life's details, the more we invite Him, the more He shows Himself strong on our behalf.

Maybe you have never had to depend on another person to brush your teeth, give you a bath, and change your undergarments, but I can tell you from experience, it is definitely humbling and begins to build the character of Christ in you. I can honestly say that I am grateful for the walk I have walked. It has poised me with grace and humility in a way that I don't think would have been obtained otherwise.

Convocation (n)-To give a summons to bishops, clergy, and delegates for an assembled special session.

Delegate (n)-A person designated to represent another. Someone who speaks or acts on the behalf of an organization (e.g., a government, a charity a trade union) at a meeting or organizations of the same level and carries out instructions from the group that sends them. They are not expected to act independently.

After being summoned to represent my country at the convocation in Jerusalem, I could not, and did not take it lightly. The Holy Spirit had directed Ruth to select me from the list that day and I wanted to do the task at hand with the upmost integrity. So I desperately prayed that day for a deep cleansing of my inner man. You must realize there are many spiritual dynamics involved here: including my heart, my soul, and body, along with the house of prayer, my church, my nation, and all that God wanted to accomplish in me, through me, and for me. Our flesh only wants comfort, satisfaction, and pleasure while our soul desires growth and significance. The only way up is down, the only way to live is to die, the only way to get is to give; we live in an upside down kingdom as far as the world is concerned. My heart's desires in writing my story is that you would be stirred to humble yourself, and become subservient to His presence, and that He would lift you up into His plans and purposes for your life.

The greatest injustice ever, is that God's creation would not serve Him with all their heart, soul, mind, and strength, after He has given us Himself in totality.

"Humble yourself (feeling very insignificant) in the presence of the Lord. And He will exalt you (He will lift you up and make your lives significant)." (James 4:10, AMP)

I believe over time, as we walk with the Lord, He gives us opportunity for self-abasement; signifying that He is the Potter and we are the clay. When our vessels our broken, we must permit ourselves to lie limp in

His hands so He can do the necessary reshaping, remembering the One who humbled Himself unto the death of the cross.

> "Therefore humble yourselves (demote, lower yourself in your own estimation) under the mighty hand of God that in due time He may exalt you." (1 Peter 5:6, AMP)

Truthfully, we all are ambassadors and delegates, in other words, representatives of God, called to carry His word in the earth. We are sanctioned by the Holy Spirit to live the gospel and preach the gospel. So how do we become humble and be an ambassador at the same time? By laying our lives down to God, and as we do that, He will pick us up and use us in a great way. We may not all go across the world, but we all are called to go across the street to our neighbors, family and friends. You may not understand the fullness of what I'm talking about, but then again you may. Possibly you have experienced a similar time in your own life. If so, embrace it!

Turn your pain into passion, your humility into holiness, and follow God to the ends of the earth, to the end of time, and throughout eternity!

Chapter 7

~ *Arrival* ~

Upon placing my feet on the foreign soul, I found it did not seem foreign at all. A friend of mine, who had been many times to Israel, told me just before leaving for this trip that when your feet touch in Israel it is like you are *home* because it is the birthplace of Jesus Christ our Lord, Savior and King. Wow what a thought! Not only is it His birthplace; it is where He grew up, where He went to school, where He started His ministry, where He was loved, where He was hated, where He was killed, where He was buried, where He was resurrected, and where He will return. Now <u>that</u> is a thought above all thoughts!

If we have made Him our Lord and Savior, through his blood, we no longer are Gentile but Jew. We have been grafted into the vine states the entire chapter of Romans eleven. We are created to love and to live as close to Jesus as possible. So, for me, going to the Son of God's home town was definitely feeling like *home* in my heart.

Now inside the Tel Aviv Airport, I found it quite different from the American airports I was accustomed to. Solders with big guns hanging over their shoulders were at every turn. We came up to a long wall of booths in which our passports were inspected. They were all speaking in another dialect which made it difficult to converse. Thankfully, through their broken English, we were able to process our personal information and we managed our way through the gate of customs.

I had never been out of the country before; it was exciting and on the other hand a little frightening. After getting through the legalities and crossing over to the outer part of the airport, my eyes began to search for a sign with a name on it; my name or the name of the convocation we were attending. The only person I knew was Ruth in all of Israel, and we were yet to meet.

There were so many people and the majority were not Americans. We breathed a sigh of relief when we found someone who spoke English and who was familiar with the hotel in Jerusalem where we had our reservations. Dear Louann had to haul around 4 large suitcases including over- the-shoulder bags, along with tending to my personal needs all at the same time. Even though she had traveled overseas many times before, she was never solely responsible for someone on such a personal level, so this added to her already full plate.

We joyfully found our transportation and were on our way to the Ramat Rachel Hotel which began our final ascent to Jerusalem-the City of the Great King. It was well over an hour and a half driving time. Leaving the big city of Tel Aviv, the only place that looked remotely like a city to me, was a journey all in itself with many twists and turns, the scenery began to change in front of my eyes. I wept at the beauty of the stone walls, hills and mountains, it seemed the very atmosphere was changing as we drew closer to Jerusalem. My heart was racing with anticipation. I truly did not know what to expect once I arrived at my destination.

After our registration papers for the hotel and the convocation were gathered; I walked hands-free alongside Louann as she got our belongings up to the sixth floor and into our room. Observing our schedules, we tried to figure out the times for the services which were written in Hebrew. I believe dinner was served from 18:00-20:30 whatever time that was, and service immediately afterwards. Together we came to a conclusion that we had approximately one hour to freshen up, eat dinner and be at the onset of the fourteen-day All Nations Convocation Jerusalem and Watchmen's Tour.

As we entered the large room where the meetings were being held, my spirit leapt at the sound of the familiar voice of Misty Edwards. She was singing a deep, worship bridal-song. The song was being played from a CD, and there were about twelve beautiful dancers who were dramatizing the song. It was the story of the ten virgins needing to fill their lamps with oil, representing the oil of intimacy with Jesus. In order to have those lamps full when the bridegroom returns, we must spend quality time with Jesus. We must *know* our bridegroom and learn to become one in the Spirit with Him. This beautiful age-old story is found in the book of Matthew 25:1-12.

Abba loves us and desires us to be completely fulfilled with His unconditional love. We can have no other love before Him. Jesus, our Bridegroom, longs for a pure bride, one that He will return for. If you flirt with the world and its sin, you are courting death, jeopardizing your future with Him and you will encounter loss; Loss of peace- loss of joy- loss of destiny.

"For I am jealous over you with godly jealousy: for I have espoused you to one husband that I may present you as a chaste virgin to Christ." (2 Corinthians 11:2, KJV)

I was overwhelmed by the anointing in the room and my heart bowed low in His majestic presence. People from all nations, tribes and tongues were there and stunningly dressed in their nation's garments, it was a beautiful sight! I felt so honored to be one of the many delegates chosen from across the world.

Tonight the shofars would sound at midnight to announce the New Year's arrival. Rosh Hashanah was setting the stage for the Yamim Nora'im or the 10 days of Awe that is commonly celebrated in the Northern Hemisphere in the autumn of the year. It is the first of the High Holy days. Rosh Hashanah is believed, by some, to be the anniversary of the day that Adam and Eve were created. Certain foods such as apples dipped in honey are used in the celebration. The Hebrew greeting for Happy New Year is *Shana Tovah* which literally means: Have a good year.

The famous violinist, Maurice Skylar was playing the song, *To Him who sits on the Throne*, on that first night. It so captivated my heart. There is nothing so graceful to my ears than the sound emanating from a skilled violinist. It was like heaven to me. Music seems to take us where mere words cannot. Someone once said; *a world without music is a mistake.* I don't know about that, but I do know that after being a psalmist for many years, and singing the scriptures along with playing the keyboard, can bring the presence of a Holy God. Each time I play and sing to an audience of *One*, or in the midst of others, my spirit lifts and I enter the realms of His glory.

The piano/keyboard is commonly called the modern day harp. A few of my secret desires are to learn to play a genuine harp and also a violin. But until then, I play the keys, and I am confident in the gifting from the Father to be a prophetic psalmist. Many decades ago I was studying on the song of the Lord, and to my astonishment I discovered that this word "psalmist" is only found once in the bible.

> **"David the son of Jesse said, and the man who was raised up high, the anointed of the God of Jacob, and the sweet psalmist of Israel, said, The spirit of the Lord spake by me and His word was on my tongue." (2 Samuel 23:1–2, KJV)**

God is raising up the true psalmist in this last day, those who will live a holy life, and allow the word of the Lord to be on their tongue. They will play skillfully with their hands; just as David did. It enthralls my heart to play it and to hear someone else who has the anointing of heaven to play and sing. It is a powerful tool to break yokes and set people free and bring refreshing.

> **"And it came to pass, when the evil spirit from God was upon Saul, that David took an harp, and played with his hand; so Saul was refreshed, and was well, and the evil spirit departed from him." (1 Samuel 16:23, KJV)**

After soaking in the sounds of Heaven for well over an hour, the speaker gave a wonderful message from the word of God. There was so much excitement filling the room. Everyone seemed to be energized by it. As my eyes scoped around the large auditorium area, I saw flags from every nation which covered all the walls, along with the most amazing banners with inspiring scripture verses and gorgeous pictures. Then I saw hundreds of people with earphones in their ears. As I turned toward the back of the room I saw many individual signs hanging over a line of tables, with the names of different countries on them. I figured out they were translators from their nation and were interpreting what was being said into a mouthpiece for them to hear. The majority of things spoken were in English, but there were songs sung in several different languages. Louann and I were trying to follow along on the big screen with some of the worship songs that were written in Hebrew, it was challenging to say the least, but very enjoyable.

As it neared midnight, the people began to gather the shofars and prepared to blow them. Anticipation filled the air. Traditionally there are a certain set of sequences in which they generally follow:

Teki'ah (long sound) Numbers 10 :3
Shevarium (three broken sounds) Numbers 10:5
Teru' ah (nine short sounds) Numbers 11:9
Teki'ah Gedolah (very long sound) Exodus 19:16,19
Shevarium Teru'ah (three broken sounds followed by nine short sounds)
The total number of blasts on Rosh Hashanah is one-hundred.

High Hosannas flooded our souls as the magnificent moment came. It is hard for me to describe how the atmosphere was charged with what felt like holy electricity. It was glorious! My soul tingled and it seemed as though this celebrated sound was going to peel the roof back and Jesus was going to appear! As the shofars sounded, some were dancing and rejoicing, others were on their faces weeping. Well over a thousand saints gave the highest honor to God in true worship. For me personally, it was an historical moment. Again, I felt so honored and humbled just to be standing among them all.

Back in our hotel room, Louann was reading the prayer delegates' schedule that we were to follow while attending the convocation. The prayer tower was set up to be going on twenty-four hours a day for the entirety of the convocation. Louann read that the United States was to cover the 04:30 time slot. So we thought we were to be in the prayer tower at 4:30 in the morning. Of course, we would be found faithful. Even after flying sixteen hours across the world, and traveling over an hour from the airport, then swallowing our food whole to make the first meeting on time, and staying in the service till after midnight; we agreed to take our place on the wall. So we slept about three hours and then got up and walked out upon the rooftop where the assigned prayer room was established. There were about seven people there when we arrived, who looked just as tired as we did. Someone was already playing the keyboard and the others were praying with great fervor. It was a holy night, and so very sweet to be in the stillness of the night, overlooking the lights of the City of the Great King… amazing, amazing! "How did I end up here Lord? I love this!"

After about forty-five minutes, we went back to our room and literally passed out with exhaustion. We had to rest and be ready for what the morrow held.

Chapter 8

~ *The Birds* ~

Rising the next morning, after Louann helped me with my grooming process, which included; bathing, brushing my teeth, styling my hair, putting on make-up and getting dressed, we headed down stairs to the hotel restaurant. Each meal was in buffet style, which meant you had to get a tray and select your food, and drink, and collect your silverware, then carry your tray to your table and eat. Well, try to imagine, if you will, Louann, having not only to retrieve all her things, but mine also. She would walk beside me as I selected what I wanted, get my drink and find us a seat among hundreds of people. Then go back in line and do it for herself. Then she would sit down huffing and puffing and cut my meat and feed me. I could not even lift a glass of water to my mouth. I do recall asking one of the servers for a straw, but he did not understand what I meant, so I don't think I ever got one. This was a very long and drawn out process that we went through three times a day. The hotel was full so the lines were very long. It seemed we were the first ones there but the last ones to leave. Patience is a wonderful virtue - is it not?

I never once heard Louann complain or say a cross word to me or anyone else. She kept herself in such a servant mode, and on top of that, she acted like she enjoyed it. Hmmmm? Anyway, she made the most mundane things that we had to deal with, tolerable and even enjoyable. Surely, God had placed her on this assignment of my journey through Jerusalem with no hands. When a person gives themselves to be in God's will, there will be joy and peace. It matters not where, when, or why.

We then made our way to the morning service. Thoughtfully, Louann asked a local about how to read the times on our schedule of events. To our relief, we discovered that the people from the United States were to lead in prayer at 4:30 in the afternoon not 4:30 in the morning. There were only around forty Americans attending the conference, which was not a lot compared to the hundreds from China and Australia, etc.

Services were being held from daylight to midnight. Myles Monroe was one of the guest speakers. He brought an extremely powerful message on the Kingdom of God that morning. Many speakers were prepared to bring us the word of the Lord from various nations. We were grateful for Tom and Kate Hess who carried the vision of the Holy Convocation. Tom and Kate were the directors of the *Jerusalem House of Prayer* which sits beautifully on top of the Mount of Olives, where we would visit in a few days. The thought of that made my heart sing!

Each prayer delegate was assigned a certain time to be in the prayer tower, which was additional to the prayers times before and after the speakers in the main auditorium. We were to pray at two-hour intervals. It was designed to go around the clock, just as the tabernacle of David did.

Twenty-four hours a day the intercessors and worshippers lifted their voices to God bringing such unity and harmony. The walls of the prayer tower on the hotel rooftop had large windows that remained open as the gentle breeze of Jerusalem swept over us. If you faced the opposite side of the tower, you would see the beauty of Bethlehem. It was absolutely breathtaking!

Now it was the first appropriate day and time for us to be in the prayer tower. The Americas, both North and South, the French, the Canadians, and people of the Islands, were in a beautiful mix of worship and song. I took my seat to play the keyboard and placed my large black braces on top to find a resting place. Uncertain if I could play the full two-hour prayer set. With the surgery barely three weeks behind me, I would have to let my fingers do all the work. Obviously, I could not play full scale in this debilitating state.

Please note that the *only thing* I was able to do with my hands was play the keyboard.

As my fingers lightly swayed across the keys, I opened my mouth and began to sing His glorious praise. The Holy Spirit within echoed His love through my voice as I burst forth a fresh new song. A few moments later, I began to notice out of the corner of my eye some birds flying around the tower. They were gray-and-black striped, stunning and graceful. We sang our worship with glorious harmony, and the louder we lifted our voices with praise; the more birds were circling the tower, well over one-hundred of them.

The leader of the group brought the room to a gentle pause and stated that even nature recognizes the high praise of God and they join in.

The room filled with the sweetest awe and you could literally see our faces being illuminated by this phenomenal fact. It brought tears to my eyes. Such joy filled my heart. I was honored to be a part of such a moment of time. As I looked down to wipe the tears from my eyes, I noticed that my shirt had the same color and design of the magnificent birds. At that precise moment the director had noticed this as well and made a comment. Wow, to be in participation with singing His praises among the nations and among nature was marvelous. When we stopped our prayer and worship, all the birds flew away. I thought, *and this is just the first day!* Regardless of my limitations, Elohim Adanai showed up, and He will do the same for you as you lift up His name with all your heart, soul, mind, and strength.

By the middle of the prayer time the burning passion to use the prophetic-psalmist gifting inside me was stirred. I began to use my teeth to remove my braces. Louann quickly came to my side to assist me; her eyes were never far from my every move. It seemed to make her nervous that I wanted to remove them, so I gave her a confident gaze that I knew what I was doing. The deep overflowing touch of Jesus was all over me and I wanted to put works with my faith. I intended on trying to play the keys with a little more flexibility and expansion. I did for about two minutes, and then I had to put the braces back on because my hands and fingers were so weak and tender. But praise God for the two minutes! I actually played full scale with no limitations!

As the prayer session ended, Louann began to gather our belongings to leave the prayer tower. One of the gentlemen approached me; he was a dark, young man from Uganda, Africa, a pastor. He began to speak with a robust African accent, "You have a well, a river dat is swelling up inside you to give to de nations. You cannot be contained! God has seen de prayer and fasting dat you have done in secret and He is going to reward you openly by sending you into prophetic rivers to de nations. You will come to my nation and have open air meetings, stadiums with large microphone. You must come and sing to officials, I will take you to Governor and I will take you to Mayor of my city. Because of de well inside it has birthed in you invitation." Looking down at my broken limbs he continued, "I don't know what happened, de Devil tried to kill you, he wanted to stop you from singing, from coming to Jerusalem, but could not. De wounds and pain are so deep and great; it is a crucifixion of you. Because you have to die, in so many areas, so He can raise you up. You have to run and give it away, and train others to pray 24/7 in de earth."

Wow, he did not know that when I had the accident three weeks before, that if my head had hit the ground first with the same velocity that my hands did, it would have cracked my skull. I could have died from the swelling of the brain. So he was accurate in saying the devil tried to kill me before I came to Jerusalem.

How many times has the enemy tried to stop us for launching forward into our God-ordained destiny? Can you recall the times when the Holy Spirit called your name? Go across the street to your sick neighbor and pray for them. Speak to the cashier at the market. Sing a happy song over that depressed person and make them smile. Give $20 to that widow. Go to a foreign country or start a church. Time after time we allow the enemy of our soul to steal some of life's greatest blessings, large or small. The devil will go to any length to stop you before you get started on any task that God has designed for you. Look at what King Herod did to try and stop Jesus from growing into His destiny; he had all the male babies killed under the age of two, in hope of destroying baby Jesus.

> **"Being warned of God in a dream they should not return to Herod, they departed into their own country another way. And when they were departed, behold, the angel of the Lord appeared to Joseph in a dream, saying, arise and take the young child and his mother and flee into Egypt, and be thou there until I bring the word: for Herod will seek the young Child to destroy him." (Matthew 2:12–16, KJV)**

Don't flee from the enemy unless you are instructed from God to do so for your safety. There might be times in which He tells you to do a certain thing or go to a certain place. Always be on guard. Listen for the instruction of the Lord.

At times, we can be our own worst enemy. We lack the courage and boldness needed to move forward in spiritual growth. These godly traits are residing on the inside each of us. But moment by moment, day by day, month after month and eventually year after year, we succumb to passivity; and we halt the moving of the Spirit of God in our lives. As we let the lesser impacting moments pass us by, we think nothing of it to concede on the greater things of God. Since we could not step into the position of a Life Group Leader, surely we could never pastor a church. If we could not pastor a church, we could not start a Fortune 500 company, or go to a third-world country to feed the poor. It is so easy to be in a trend of *unrelenting* that we miss the small and the large opportunities. Then at the end of our life's journey we leave no legacy for others to follow. Nor would we be able to give our lives in martyrdom if need be; all because we did not give ourselves away for the cause of Christ. We grow accustomed to giving in to the fleshly desires, that when the Holy Spirit moves on us to do something, we turn the other way. The statement is true, *If we cannot live for Christ, we could not die for Him either.*

As we have no ambition to change our world around us, we are not able to obtain the drive to do exploits in His Name. At this point, Satan hooks up to our lethargic spirits and we end up living in a rut of selfishness, then dying, unfortunately leaving no mark on mankind of what Jesus could have done through us. I encourage you to begin to dream the dream of God and to rise up and answer the call He has placed on your life. If I could fly across the world with two broken limbs, when most people would not even go across town, surely you can heed and obey what God calls you to do. Free up yourself by allowing the Holy Spirit to lead you in to the greater things of life. I long to be free as those birds in the sky that day that were circling the prayer tower in my expression of worship and service to my Creator.

Chapter 9

~ *Praying at the Jaffa Gate* ~

At the convocation the next day, over a thousand people gathered to hear the word of the Lord and to pray. There was a psalmist of Israel who began to play his beautiful harp; He would sing the scriptures in English and then tell us the words in Hebrew so we could join in song. It was an amazing sound as we all began to sing in one language. The sweet sound escalated higher and higher as we declared that Jehovah would set us up high upon a rock and hide us in the cleft of that rock. Then people began to sing out in their heavenly language. This went on for over thirty minutes as Jehovah Nissi, the Lord our Banner, was lifted among the nations gathered. Dancers began to step out of their seats and began to be moved by the Holy Spirit. I witnessed the Chinese, the Jamaicans, and the Jewish, etc... wonderfully display their love to our Redeemer and Life Giver. Then the speaker, Heidi Baker, opened her mouth and heart and began to speak of the Faithful Witness and His faithfulness to her and her family. She invited Yeshua into the lives of everyone present and beckoned us to enter into the rest of God. She kept repeating the words, "Get low, go slow. Get low, go slow. Bow in humility before God as we press into Him." She beckoned us to enter the rest of God and not to rush what He wanted to do, and to walk humbly in the timing of the Lord, and to be still enough to hear His commands. "*Shma Yisrael Adonai Eloheynu, Adonai Echad*"

After the morning session, the American, the Canadian and the French teams, headed toward the Jaffa Gate to pray. There were about forty-five of us ecstatically going to the Old City. On the transit bus, the psalmist who was playing the harp in the main services, was among us. From the back of the bus, he played his beautiful harp. He strummed a lovely song, and off his tongue rolled the song of the Lord; the entire bus became heavenly.

What a divine ride. Once we arrived at our destination, all of us walked through the streets of Jerusalem to our designated meeting place which was the *Christ Church,* believed to be the oldest Protestant congregation in the Middle East. Churches in Jerusalem are more commonly called *Congregations* or *Synagogues,* unlike in America where we may call it the *Church of God* or *Assembly of God.*

This exquisite, ancient building was filled to capacity, with people standing along the walls just to be a part of the prayer service. The room temperature was hot due to no air conditioning, and the fire of God made it even hotter. A passionate fire began to burn inside me for the apple of God's eye; Jerusalem and her people. But more intensely, the zealous flame was for our Messiah.

Many people spoke that day and gave testimony of His greatness. There was a young Jewish couple sharing their story of how Yeshua had called them to sell out completely; to leave their secular jobs, and minister in His Name. She was great with child and seemed stunningly pure of heart. My mind was seeing them as the notable Joseph and Mary; tears splashed down my face and onto my clothing as they enlightened us all with the glories of heaven.

I met people in that room that spoke precisely to my heart. One of them was Ann; a tall, slender, precious lady from England. She approached me and asked me to pray for her cheek bone. She had fallen down prior to making her way to Israel. The left side of her face was badly bruised. After I declared healing over her, I told her of my fall as well. Instantly out of her mouth she spoke these words, "Do you not know you are on a special assignment from heaven? Do you not know that God has appointed you to be here and nothing could have stopped you?" I was so humbled with these words from the Father's heart. We embraced and she thanked me profusely for not giving in to pain and limitation, for pressing on to the mark that was evidently laid out for me.

Stepping outside, another lovely lady, who I recognized from the hotel, reached out and took my arm and said, "You ministered to me through the song of the Lord. The Messiah pressed me to tell you that when these braces come off your hands you are going to have a completely different sound; a powerful and mighty anointing, which will be fresh and new." Sobbing graciously, I fell into her embrace. After wiping away our tears, Rachel and I began to converse as the group leader was walking us toward our final destination; the *Jaffa Gate.* I told her my daughter's name was Leah, referring to Jacob in the scriptures who married Rachel and Leah.

"And Laban had two daughters; the name of the elder was Leah and the name of the younger was Rachel." (Genesis 30:16–18, KJV)

Then I shared that my Leah had a beautiful new baby named Anna, named after the prophetess/intercessor in the scripture. Rachel then informed me that her granddaughter was named Leah and her great granddaughter was named Anna. Needless to say, Rachel and I had an instant connection and many spiritual dynamics came to light as we spent more time together throughout the remainder of our stay in the city of the Great King.

Standing in the shadow of the Jaffa Gate; a magnificent stone wall which had an open portal into the Old City Jerusalem, I breathed a deep gratifying sigh.

The Jaffa Gate is only one of the gates established centuries ago throughout the city. The gateway towers twenty-feet high, and the wall that it is attached to is mounted another twenty-feet above that. Absolutely breathtaking!

It is also called by some, David's Gate. The tower of David, the Citadel, is located near within sight. The Jaffa Gate faces to the west, which is in the direction of the United States of America (my home land), Canada, and France. The psalmist set up his large harp and I began to sing and pray prophetically for my country. The main reason for which I was invited to come here in the first place; destiny had called my name, and I had answered. I commenced to speak prophetically in the atmosphere. I proclaimed that His Kingdom come, His will be done, on earth as it is in Heaven. I declared holiness, righteousness and justice over my country and peace over Jerusalem. It seemed the authority from the throne was being piped through my earthen vessel. This indeed was a weighty moment; only eternity will reveal what transpired at the Jaffa Gate that day. Our prayers are weighty anytime, anywhere we decisively give ourselves to them. We do not have to be standing at the Jaffa Gate, per se, we just have to stand in our position in Christ.

Once we have given ourselves to Him we have authority to use His Name. It is God's plan that we pray for others.

> **"I exhort therefore, that first of all, supplications, prayers, intercession, and giving of thanks, be made for all men; For kings, and for all that are in authority; that we made lead a quiet and peaceable life in all godliness and honesty." (1 Timothy 2:1–2, KJV)**

After our prayer time was finished, our team walked toward the place to board our public transportation. While I rested on a small, crumpled piece of a wall, about a dozen people from France began to gather around me. They were talking in French so I did not know a word they were speaking, but I sensed that they wanted to pray for my arms. It was priceless as each one of them gently laid hands on me and prayed sincerely in their French dialect. I hugged them all and thanked them for their tenderness and compassion toward me. This ordained moment united us in a way that I cannot explain. God was putting the nations in my heart and I felt the capacity enlarging. What a sweet interval indeed.

A person I recently met, who lives in Israel, told me that if you could see the nations through the *eyes of Israel* first, it would bring proper alignment of the *heart of Jesus* into your heart. This was definitely happening to me, it is becoming a distinct measure of time of which I am grateful.

If you have not had the privilege of letting your feet walk in the Land of the Bible, and you feel there is nothing awaiting you here, let me say to the heart that is numb- and the tongue that is dumb- the Bridegroom calls you to come... Come to Jerusalem!

> **"Our feet shall stand within they gates,
> O Jerusalem."** (Psalms 122:2, KJV)

> **"I am the Gate; whoever enters through Me will be saved. They
> will come in and out and find pasture."** (John 10:9, NIV)

The eye-catching stone walls and buildings that surrounded the city are made with Jerusalem limestone. By law, this must be used to prevent architectural competition with the Old City. I found it most intriguing that within Jerusalem most of the government and administration buildings are located, such as Parliament and the Supreme Court. Jesus loves all inhabitants of the earth and desires to be our King, ruling and reigning over our lives.

> **"For unto us a child is born, unto us a Son is given; and the
> government will be upon his shoulder. And His name will
> be called Wonderful, Counselor, Mighty God, Everlasting
> Father, Prince of Peace. Of the increase of his government
> and peace there will be no end, upon the throne of David, and
> over His kingdom, to order it, and establish with it judgment
> and justice from that time forward, even forever. The zeal of
> the Lord of hosts will perform this."** (Isaiah 9:6–7, NKJV)

Government is released through our intercession. Declaring the word of God out of a pure heart establishes that His Kingdom will reign on the earth. It moves the heart of God when we speak His word back to Him in prayer; doing this is the most powerful dynamic in the earth today. Intercession is coming into agreement with what God has promised in His word. The Father has ordained that *His House; His people*, rule with Jesus through intimacy-based intercession. Intimacy refs to how the heart connects with God. He governs the universe in partnership with His people. He opens doors of blessings and closes doors of oppression in response to our prayers.

> "Will not God bring about justice for his chosen ones, who cry out day and night? Will He keep putting them off?" (Luke 18:7, NIV)

The answer is *yes*, He will bring justice, and *no*, He will not put us off. This is why we must rise to a pure place of a true lifestyle of intercession; it should be based out of our love for God and love for His creation.

> "And pray in the Spirit on all occasions with all kinds of prayers and requests. With this in mind, be alert and always keep on praying for the Lord's people." (Ephesians 6:18, NIV)

Back at the hotel, after dinner, many of us were resting outside in the plaza area. Louann and I found seats with an elderly French woman. We had spoken with her on occasion up in the prayer tower. She shared how she had been to Israel several times from France, teaming up with the Jerusalem House of Prayer. Each time helping to give French translation during convocation services and also in the prayer room. You could not help but see her zealousness for Jesus as she prayed for her country. Corrie* was born in a small town just outside of Paris. She gave recollection to being hidden from the war in a suburb of Paris by her father until she was around the age of four. She had a half-sister who was of a different nationality. This sister would persecute her, and would tell her father that Corrie's new found faith had engaged her in a cult. Life was extremely difficult, but she pressed through the persecution and grew into an amazing woman of God. Not only did she learn the scriptures, she also learned to speak in four different languages. This is no small task. After marriage, she and her husband ministered abroad. She shared that he would teach the Bible, and she would move as a prophetic intercessor. Later she became the vice president of the *Paris Women's Aglow*, which gave her a platform to reach many souls. While in

France, her and her husband attended a *Word of Faith Church*, and had previously attended Kenneth Hagen's *Rhema Bible School*. Interestingly, she also translated books for an American author named *Jim Goll*; and would work hard putting writings into the French language. I was fortunate to have read one of his books on intercession, and to have met him a nearby city in Florida. Corrie quickly became our dear friend and remains so until this day. Louann and I were given a personal invitation to France to stay in her home. Part of the calling on her life involves circulating American Christians throughout France. Yet another divine connection indeed; what an amazing God we serve.

While in conversation with our friend Corrie, I noticed out of the corner of my eye a handsome and very tall, blonde-haired, young man curiously glancing at me. When I had finished speaking with Corrie, I noticed he was making his way toward me. This young man stood head and shoulder above other men. My eyes naturally looked at the name tag he was wearing on his shirt which read, *Jonathan-United States*. To open the conversation I said, "USA? Which state are you from?" As he was telling me his home town in Texas, I found myself telling him I was from Lakeland, Florida. With a huge grin on his face he said, "I work with Lance Wallnau Ministries and we are travelling to Lakeland, Florida in a few months to minister in a church there." "What church?" I enquired. When he named my home church's name, I almost fell over with surprise and delight! He then told me that they had met a man named Everett Hamilton, from *Kingdom Business Network*, and he had extended the invitation for their ministry to come to our church. Amazingly, Everett and his wife Mary have been dear friends of mine for many years. Here I am standing in Jerusalem, Israel and I meet a perfect stranger who tells me he is scheduled to be in *my* church back in the USA. There are seven billion people on the planet and probably half as many churches and he is coming to mine! It's a small world after all!

The reason Jonathan had been gazing at me earlier, was because he was compelled by the Holy Spirit to lay hands on my wounded arms and speak healing. First, he thanked me for my obedience to come to Israel with all the physical challenges; this tenderly touched my heart. Then he spoke of how the disciples were told to lay hands on the sick and they would recover. Jonathan wanted to do the same thing. He stated that the fire of God would burn out the metal in my wrists for complete recovery. He told me that I was not a person *influenced by people* around me, but that *I am the influence* when around people. He declared that I was called to do exploits in His name. I felt the presence of God come and blow over me. He also stated that there was a release of angelic hosts around me to keep me steady; and I was granted wisdom and revelation because I had asked for it. In quoting Isaiah, he announced that I would hear God's voice behind me saying; *this is the way walk ye in it.*

> "And thine ears shall hear a word behind thee, saying, 'This is the way, walk ye in it, when ye turn to the right hand, and when ye turn to the left.'" (Isaiah 30:21, KJV)

You must understand that I am not a person of deity any more than you are; just an earthen vessel wanting Jesus in my life, hungry for His plan to unfold. Indeed God touched me gloriously that day with His healing balm, new friendships, godly surprises, invitations to foreign lands, singing with one of Israel's true psalmists, and hearing God's voice through His servants. Why shouldn't God, being an all-consuming fire, burn the metal right out of my wrists? All things are possible to him who believes.

What a day filled with the Glory of His majesty; the prayers, the Jaffa Gate, the people, the diversity, I prized it all.

* Due to the sensitive nature of the ministry, the name has been changed.

Chapter 10

~ *Bethlehem–Place of the Nativity* ~

———— ·ᵛᵛᵛ∘◦◖◗◦◦◖◗◦◦ᵛᵛᵛ· ————

Late one night a knock came on our hotel door. Louann and I looked questionably at one another as she slowly went to the door and asked who it was. The unfamiliar voice said, "Ruth." She slowly opened the door and there were two smiling women whose faces were beaming. It was the lady who had called my church that day and invited me to come to Israel. I was so pleased to meet her and her dear friend Darla. She had come to check on our room accommodations, but primarily wanted to check on my broken arms. Ruth was encouraged by how I put forth so much effort to still come to the convocation. After I told her of the accident, she thought I would decline the invitation. No! Through the calamity, I learned to cling tighter to God, it surely wasn't easy, but I didn't need easy; just possible. In the brief time the four of us shared, I identified the like-precious faith between us.

> "Simon Peter a servant and an apostle of Jesus
> Christ, to them who have obtained like precious
> faith with us through the righteousness of God and
> our savior Jesus Christ." (2 Peter 1:1, KJV)

Ruth kindly asked if they could pray for my recovery. After the heartfelt prayer; they both began to speak by the Holy Spirit saying that God had called me to Jerusalem *for such a time as this.* Adding yet another treasurable confirmation that I should be here.

Before they left, I told them how my heart's desire was to swim in the Sea of Galilee. Ruth educated us by telling that it was a six-hour drive one way. Gladly they offered to drive us there. Furthermore she told us that the two of them would take us anywhere we wanted to go. She encouraged us to pray, and ask God where He wanted us, then make a list for them so they could schedule their days. When Ruth and Darla left our room that night, we stood amazed at the favor we had been shown. I mean, how many people do you know who live in Israel and would personally take you anywhere you desired to go? This was huge!

One of the first places we wanted to go was Bethlehem, the birth place of Jesus. Charmingly, both Ruth and Darla lived in Bethlehem; which is just south of Jerusalem.

Ruth could not accompany us on the first day, so, as the three of us made our way to the *gate of customs* to enter into the city of Bethlehem. After allowing them to view our passports, we entered, and my eyes scoped out this very lowly, humble city where my Lord Jesus Christ was born. It was much different than Jerusalem. Some of the streets were lined with rubbish and debris. It's somewhat remarkable that Bethlehem had not really changed through the years; it is as lowly, humble place.

On the way to view the Nativity, Darla took us to a friend who owned a local restaurant. Interestingly, the word *Bethlehem* means in modern terms: *house of bread*.

Once we entered the humble yet beautiful building, the owners of the restaurant took us down a stairwell, which went to a back room; this is where he seated only very special guests. He began to serve us handmade delicacies from his city. We were given the very best there was available, and were treated like royalty. I must add that this meal was the very best I had tasted since arriving in Israel; it was positively delicious.

I felt so comfortable and satisfied, not only with the food and my surroundings, but with the servant-hood of the people. We had been obliged with genuine humility and gratitude. The owner was honored that we were there under his roof, and the feelings were mutual.

I couldn't help but think about Joseph and Mary as they knocked on doors looking for a place to birth baby Jesus, yet they found *no* welcome. Upon leaving the restaurant, we strolled inside a few local shops, where

I bought my husband a pair of handcrafted sandals, with the name Bethlehem written across the souls. I could never attain them in the United States. Surely Phillip will feel like he is walking the dusty streets here with them on. Happily, I found a gorgeous hand-made tambourine that could be play in our house of prayer. The things the people make are astounding; it was a joy to bring these small treasures home with me.

Many people were in the streets as we made our way to the *Church of the Nativity*. There seemed to be a different atmosphere than in the other places we had visited; maybe because the majority of people that live here are Muslims.

Darla guided us through a small door in which you had to actually bow down to enter. This entry led to the Church of the Nativity which is built on top of where tradition says, is the place of Jesus's birth. Carefully we wobbled down a narrow spiral staircase that descended to the place where Christ was born. Stepping inside the area, I noticed a lady laying prostrate with her face near a small opening in the floor. She lay there quite some time, and I wondered what she was doing. When she finished and had left the room, I walked toward what looked like a golden flower of some sort with a hole of about six or eight inches in the center. There was what seemed like a shrine made over the top of where baby Jesus laid for its preservation. I felt so honored to be standing in the same spot where Mary and Joseph came to deliver the Son of the Living God. Even though it looked nothing like I had imagined; I bowed my knees and stretched out prostrate over the place of his birth. I and inhaled where He drew His first breath and I had this thought; *this is where the Lord of all Creation, Jesus the Christ took his very **first human breath***. The Spirit of the Lord descended heavily; I could barely lift the weight of my own body off of the floor. The breath of the Holy One of Israel had pierced my lungs, I would never be the same after this holy encounter. Tranquility was like liquid pouring over me. Calmly, with great reverence, I arose and made my ascent up the stairwell to leave this sacred sight. Please don't misconstrue what I am saying here. The shrine that covered the place were baby Jesus could have been born was not holy in itself. The touch I sensed from the Lord was because, in my mind, I put myself in the manger scene with Mary, Joseph and Jesus. I tried to relive the event as I lay there on my face. I visualized baby Jesus drawing His first breath.

God has given us imaginations for our benefit not our detriment. Let me instruct you to tap into this wonderful gift that the Creator of the Universe has giving you, it can be delightfully powerful.

Darla, Louann, and I, strolled through the promenade of her home town, Bethlehem, enjoying the dynamics of the city. Shortly after this, Darla took us to her abode, where her family lived in a large apartment along with Ruth and her family. Their children were laughing as we entered the door and were introduced to their husbands. Life was teeming out of us all; what a night of splendid joy as we sat in the living room and fellowshipped. God had aligned us with these precious true friends that will forever live our hearts.

Over on a small table I saw a beautiful harp; it seemed it was crying for me to caress it; I softly asked if I could play it, "yes of course," was their reply. One of the children placed the harp between my knees as I gingerly strummed the strings. I closed my eyes and thought on His Faithfulness. I found it exhilarating to be in Bethlehem playing such a purposeful instrument like David did in his lifetime.

"One of the servants said, "I've seen someone who knows how to play the harp. He is a son of Jesse from Bethlehem. He's a brave man. He would make a good solider. He's a good speaker. He's very handsome. And the Lord is with him." Then Saul sent messengers to Jesse. He said, "Send me your son David, the one who takes care of your sheep." (I Samuel 16:18–19, NIRV)

Night began to fall and I imagined David, as a shepherd boy, playing his harp to lull the sheep to a restful sleep. My journey in Bethlehem was just as exhilarating as my journey in Jerusalem! Here I am, in my dear friend's home with their families, playing on this amazing instrument, listening to all the children laughing joyfully; what great peace! The degree of joy was beyond measure.

Darla and Ruth took me through the apartment. As we entered one of the bedrooms, I saw another door in the room. Then, to my surprise, they escorted me onto a small balcony. Standing there in dazzling splendor of the starlight sky, how could I not think of the *Star of Bethlehem* which led the three wise men to Jesus' birth?

> "Now when Jesus was born in Bethlehem of Judea in the days of Herod the king, behold, there came wise men from the east to Jerusalem, saying, Where is he that is born King of the Jews? For we have seen his star in the east, and are come to worship him." (Matthew 2:1–2, KJV)

Awestruck in the moment, I thought, *can this wonderful journey get any better?*

Darla then pointed at the field below and said, "This was the actual field of Boaz, where Ruth gleaned from him."

> "And Ruth went and gleaned in a field after the reapers; and she happened to stop at the field belonging to Boaz, who was of the family of Elimelec." (Ruth 2:3, AMP)

Amazing! I wept, it all seemed too good to be true. My eyes slowly scanned the landscape, while with my imagination, I pictured the two Bible characters living their everyday lives so many centuries ago. What a privilege is was to be standing in this spot. Each day in Israel was more precious than the day before. In my heart I thought, *I may never pass this way again, so I'll hold onto these sacred memories and keep them inside of me forever.*

Loading into the car, Ruth, Louann, and I, began to make our way back to our hotel in Jerusalem. Wanting to give us the desires of our hearts, Ruth side-tracked our route and drove down some cobblestone streets and narrow alleys; she was searching for a friend of hers that made sweet-smelling anointing oils. Before I left the United States, several of our friends from the house of prayer and the healing room at my local church had given me money; they wanted me to purchase anointing oils to fulfill the scripture.

> "Is any sick among you? Let him call for the elders of the church; and let them pray over him, anointing him with oil in the name of the Lord." (James 5:15, KJV)

> "I have found David my servant; with my holy oil have I anointed him." (Psalms 89:20 KJV)

We parked the car, and walked into a tiny back room where a kind, elderly man was seated. We were amazed at the rows of boxes and empty bottles. There were very large, medium-sized, and some small bottles. In separate bottles he had many fragrances such as Rose of Sharon, Lily of the Valley, etc. He began to tell us how he spends his days mixing oils and fragrances to create the highly demanded anointing oils. We were captivated as he made the sizes and fragrances that we requested.

With my eyes I saw an ancient way of making and bottling anointing oil. This was not a factory with machines racing to manufacture them, but a tender-eyed gentleman that had made a modest living with his trade. It touched my heart because the world I live in back in the United States was nowhere close to this; it was truly a valuable sight.

After Louann and I purchased all the oil we could possibly carry back on the plane, we genuinely thanked the man, then made our way back to our hotel. What a day of whiffing the indigenous aromas of Bethlehem and observing it as well.

Chapter 11

~ *The Western Wall* ~

Louann and I had joined up with a precious pastor from India named Esua. I had originally met him in one of the morning services of the convocation. It was at a time in the service when people went forward to the altar to pray. While seated alone, I was waiting for Louann to return from the altar, when I noticed a dark, middle-aged man turning around in his seat to look my way. He did this several times, and then he got up and approached me. In his broken English, he proceeded to tell me that God had directed him to come and talk to me. He then handed me a beautiful color brochure of his ministry in India. As I leafed through its pages, I said, "I notice you are building a prayer tower?" "Yes," he replied, "And I am asking God for intercessors." he added. "That is what I am and this is what I do!" I replied. "I know, you will come to my village, to our wooden prayer tower and teach my people to pray. I have a small keyboard there and a place for you to rest your head," he matter-of-factly stated. He then proceeded in showing me more pictures of the wooden prayer tower being built there in India. I was inundated by the words he spoke. Shortly, Louann made her way back from the altar and I introduced her to Pastor Esua. Our conversation took on such a beautiful form as I sensed a tender friendship was in the making. Louann shared with him about her many trips to India, and how she loved the people, and wanted to return. As the two of them engrossed in further conversation, I began thinking, *how did he know I was an intercessor and played the keyboard as*

I prayed? I had never laid eyes on him before. This thought moved me to tears; only time will tell where this relationship will lead us.

Louann, Pastor Esua, and I, headed out to view the ancient city. Our transportation dropped us off on a curbed area overlooking Jerusalem. I walked away from my two friends to be alone. I wondered if this could have been the very spot where Jesus stood and wept over the city, His city.

> **"Oh Jerusalem, Jerusalem thou that killeth the prophets, and stonest them which are sent unto thee; how often would I have gathered thy children, even as a hen gathers her chickens under her wings, and ye would not!"** (Matthew 23:27, KJV)

As I pictured my Savior here weeping for His people, my own tears were unstoppable and my heart was beckoning God's chosen people to come under His wings. My mouth opened and out came, "Oh Jerusalem, come to your Messiah, come to your King!" With my voice carried by the wind, I sang prophetically even more forcefully, "I call you Oh Jerusalem, for His return is near. He will set His feet on the Mount of Olives and rule and reign for 1000 years from this Great City. Come! Oh Jerusalem! I call you! Hear His cry today and you will know your God and you will come to your King of Kings, your Lord of Lords!" My soul was heavy for the inhabitants of Jerusalem that I could scarcely carry myself. I did not want to leave this place for all eternity! I was overwhelmed; I had never experienced such a love like this before. It seemed to intrinsically intoxicate me. My heart was captured with great love and passion for Jerusalem and God's chosen people! I shall never forget that half-hour for the rest of my life; it changed me-The city of the Great King!

As I tore myself away from the intensity of praying for our Messiah's people, we began to walk down into a small valley and then up high on another hill. It was a little strenuous to walk on and the heat was bearing down on us. I asked Louann for a drink of water and she opened the water bottle for me placing it between my two braces, as she had done about a hundred times before. I very carefully lifted it to my mouth and took a long drink. It was going to be a long, hot, but thrilling day.

The city is divided into four parts: the Muslim Quarter, Christian Quarter, Jewish Quarter and the American Quarter. I was intrigued by being able to walk from one Quarter to another, and see the significant differences of each one. I found it to be absolutely amazing. It was like turning the pages of a book and viewing a completely different scene on each page.

We tread on streets where there were more people walking than cars driving. The buildings and artifacts all around us were fascinating. We passed the *Tower of David* which was just across the street from the *Jaffa Gate*. As we rounded the corner, there were hundreds of vendors with wide open doors. This market place, which resembled a mall, is where you could purchase a myriad of treasures from any one of the stores. With *my eyes only* could I look upon all the beautiful Jerusalem treasures and trinkets. I was not able to pick up anything to analyze it because my fingers could not grip or my hands bear weight. It was difficult restraining myself from handling things that I knew I may never be able to see again.

Standing in the doorway of one of the stores, Louann told me to wait there with Pastor Esua as she stepped a few doors down for a quick peek. I obeyed, but within minutes, Pastor Esua had left also; leaving me alone in the store with just the owner. Abruptly, the owner began to scream, "Move back, move back to the back of the store!" As we shuffled about, I almost lost my balance and was confused at why he was doing this. Unexpectedly, over a loudspeaker, I heard a man speaking in Hebrew. Then I saw two military vans drive up, and parked next door, then about thirty-five men in green uniforms quickly got out. Hurriedly they made the people who were walking in the streets get out of the way. All of sudden, I heard a loud boom, then another and another, until the sound repeated four times. Making my way closer to the store's entrance and peering out, I saw yellow tape being draped across the store-front just two doors down. Someone found four bombs and the military came to detonate them. My heart was racing by this time and I did not know what would happen next. Shrieking I said, "Where is Louann? Where is Louann?" She came strolling slowly down the street, taking her sweet time, admiring the sites and finally walked into the store where she had left me. I said, "Did you hear the bombs?" "What bombs? Are you joking?" she said. "No!" I exclaimed. Where she had been positioned, there was loud music playing and she didn't hear a thing. It was a crazy and scary moment and she missed all the action. We both exhaled a huge sigh of relief, and then laughed to keep from crying. Leaning my head on her shoulder, I whimpered, "Don't leave me again!"

Joining back up with our friend, Pastor Esua, we headed toward the *Wailing Wall* or more commonly called the *Western Wall*. I began to sing in the Spirit while walking toward the entrance. Having a Davidic tone in my voice I began to sing, *I'm on my way to the Western Wailing Wall; to insert the names of the ones I love; to the Western Wall to give a holy prayer unto my God.*

This ancient site is founded in the Old City of Jerusalem, dwelling at the base on the west side of the *Temple Mount*. It magnificently stands over one-hundred feet tall. People from all across the earth come to partake in the beauty of its history. After reaching the entry way to the Wall, we had to go through a guarded area to be searched by the security officials. I ignorantly had across my shoulders a tallit; a prayer shawl that is a ritual garment in which the fringes reminds the wearer of the commandments of the Torah; which is the first five books of the Bible. Louann had brought it from our church's house of prayer. Our intention was to wear the tallit to the Wall and pray for our friends and family at home, knowing that the anointing is transferrable according to scripture found in the book of Acts.

"So that from his body were brought unto the sick handkerchiefs or aprons, and the diseases departed from them, and the evil spirits went from them." (Acts 19:12, KJV)

We believed the sweet anointing would filter through the cloth and then we would carry it back to the States. Unfortunately, we did not know that women are not permitted to wear a tallit in public. The guard who was attending this area showed annoyance on his face as he signaled for me take it off and place it in my bag, out of view of the people. This shows how much that I need to learn of the Jewish customs. But

I guarantee that when I return to Israel someday, I will have not have forgotten the sacredness of this custom; along with the uneasiness I felt while near the soldier with the gun strapped across his shoulder.

Upon entering what is called the *Western Wall Plaza*; I saw a large open area with hundreds of orthodox Jews and young children in school uniforms close to the Wall. Other people were mingled in as well. I walked toward a large metal sign and began to read these words:

THE DIVINE PRESENCE NEVER MOVES FROM THE WESTERN WALL

Jewish tradition teaches that the Temple Mount is the focal point of Creation. In the center of the mountain lies the Foundation Stone of the world. Here Adam came into being, here Abraham, Isaac and Jacob served God. The First and Second Temples were built upon this mountain. The Ark of the Covenant was set up on the foundation stone itself. Jerusalem was chosen by God as the dwelling place of the Shechinah. David longed to build the Temple and Solomon his son built the first Temple here about 3000 years ago. The Second Temple was destroyed by the Nebucazzerite of Babylon and was rebuilt on its ruins 70 years later. The present Western Wall before you is a remnant of the Western Temple Mount retaining walls. Jews have prayed in its shadow for hundreds of years, an expression of their faith and the rebuilding of the Temple. The Sages said about it: The Divine Presence never moves from the Western Wall. The Temple Mount continues to be the focus of prayer for Jews from all over the world.
"MY HOUSE IS A HOUSE OF PRAYER FOR ALL PEOPLES" (Isaiah 56:7, KJV).

Warm tears streamed down my cheeks as I read these words for it seemed as if I was standing in the most holy place of all on the earth and I guess I was.

Imagine standing in the place where possibly *Adam and Eve* were created. It was mind boggling. Also the place where the *Ark of the Covenant* was laid; *holy* was the only word on my lips.

My mind could barely fathom the thought of me, Janet Penney, from Lakeland Florida, actually standing in this place. I wanted to lay prostrate on my face and weep perpetually.

Built by King Herod in 20 BC, the Temple Mount is considered the holiest of Jewish sites in all of Jerusalem. This large open area, called *The Plaza*, functions as an open-air synagogue that can accommodate tens of thousands of worshipers. Prayer takes place day and night around the wall and also many bar mitzvahs are held here as well. Everyone is welcome.

When facing the Wall; the prayers of the people must remain silent. As I slowly took steps toward this magnificent place, I noticed a large dividing screen separating the men's area from the women's area; which is Jewish custom. All men must have a type of head covering, which are freely provided in a box at the entrance of the prayer area. Also, in another box, was provided covering for women. They were to cover their arms, or if they were wearing shorter apparel; their legs must also be covered to honor the Orthodox Jewish tradition.

Before drawing near the Wall, the people were to cleanse their hands with the provided large, round laver with about seven spouts. This is a ceremonial ablution in the ancient Jewish Tabernacle and Temple worship.

As I approached the wall, I noticed many Orthodox Jews dressed in black pants, black vest, black hats, and coats, and they were swaying back and forth in front of the Wall and chanting. They were softly reciting from the book of Psalms.

I glanced to my far right on the women's side of the wall, and there a shelf contained many Hebrew Bibles. I made my way over and affectionately picked one up with my elbows and was straining as I embraced it to my chest. Even though I could not read the Hebrew writing, my eyes absorbed the beautiful script.

Louann tenderly placed a small piece of paper and a pen in between my fingers. This was the very first time I used my hands to write since the accident. Still yet another seemingly small challenge of being on this journey with no functioning hands. In this most holy place on the planet; Jehovah Jirah, my Provider, was providing strength for my weak fingers.

I took the pen and wrote the names of my loved ones and it more than a bit challenging. Before I left the United States, I only had two sessions of physical therapy because I was leaving to come here to Israel in a matter of days. Those two short sessions were not near enough, but joyfully, this was helping. I will always recall that I had a physical therapy session at the historic *Western Wall!*

Once you reach the yellowish-white, chalky blocks of the wall, you will notice the small cracks and crevices within its stature. Over the centuries of time, people just like myself, have come and placed their prayer requests on bits of paper then stuffed them into the cracks. This being an ancient tradition, the wall was covered with tidbits of paper. I was determined to use my fingers to wiggle the small paper into a tiny crack. Affectionately, I placed my hand on top of it as I thought of my family and friends and of the divine intervention they needed. Silently, I began to pray. Within a few short minutes, the Holy Spirit was groaning within me; the travailing of my heart was superior above any other prayer moments I had lived out. It was as if time had stood still. I felt like my entire being was attached somehow to this Wall. Completely saturated with the Shekinah Glory of God, I *could not* move my body, I *did not* want to move my body. Literally hundreds of thousands of people stood praying in this exact spot, and possibly, Adam and Eve who walked with God in the cool of the day.

> **"And they heard the voice of Lord God walking in the garden in the cool of the day." (Genesis 3:8, kjv)**

Think about it; human history began in a prayer meeting. In this frame of mind and spirit, I was not aware of how much time had elapsed with me hugging this wall. It seemed like I was in eternity, almost like an out-of-body experience. Before long, I sensed Louann behind me. She softly placed her hand on top of mine as we joined in prayer at the holiest site in all the world.

There were hundreds of people lined up behind us waiting their turn to draw close. So in respect of time and people, I peeled myself off of the wall and began to slowly walk backwards. It is told that you should never turn your back on the Glory of God; so following the lead of others, very carefully we backed our way out. My lips were uttering this prayer; "Let me never turn my back on Your Glory, Oh God, let me never turn my back on Your Glory." Transformed by this encounter; I wept profusely as we found our way to exit the Plaza, but to never exit from His Divine Presence.

Chapter 12

~ *City of David* ~

Walking down a small cobblestone road in the City of David; Darla, Louann, and I, made our way to a small, underground prayer room. Darla introduced us to a lovely, elderly woman with silver hair arranged beautifully in a small bun. My affection developed quickly as I discerned that this woman was soaked in prayer. She had been leading this house of prayer for over ten years. The room itself was exceedingly magnificent and full of glory. There were banners, flags, swords, shields, and Hebrew writings along all the walls. Along one wall there was a small area made for a private place of prayer; a canopy with white tulle and other materials. This arrangement is commonly called a huppah or chupah in a Jewish wedding.

This precious saint led me to an exquisite keyboard and sat me down to enter into a time of worship and prayer. There were about eight people joining us. She politely told me that I must play and sing softly because several Muslim families lived on the floor just above us. I did exactly as I was instructed. The sweet presence of the Holy One of Israel increased as we all began to pray. Sitting the this holy place in the real city of *David*, the only psalmist listed in scripture, the man after God's heart, the King of Israel; I was awestruck to have been given this privilege.

"And David spake to the chief of the Levites to appoint their brethren to be the singers with instruments of music, psalteries and harps and cymbals, sounding, by lifting up the voice of joy." (1 Chronicles 15:16, KJV)

A prophetic sound of joy continuously poured forth from my lips; decreeing peace and prosperity over all the families of Israel.

> "And said unto the Levites that taught all Israel, which were holy unto the Lord, put the holy ark in the house which Solomon the son of David king of Israel did build; it shall not be a burden upon your shoulders: serve now the Lord your God, and his people Israel, and prepare yourselves by the houses of your fathers, after your courses, according to the writing of David king of Israel, and according to the writing of Solomon his son. And stand in the holy place according to the divisions of the families of the fathers of your brethren the people, and after the division of the families of the Levites." (2 Chronicles 35:3–5, KJV)

Even though my wrists were broken my hands remained intact, weak but intact; nothing could stop me from ministering unto my God. Graced for over an hour to softly play, I then eased to a gentle halt, then turned on the bench and peacefully slid down to the floor and laid prostrate in the presence of the Lord. I could feel the prayers that had been ascending from this house over the past decade of time. Prevailing richness and purity pureness had never been within my grasp before. Oh how these people loved our Messiah! They had abandoned their lives to Him, and they had no other love. Elohim Adonai is their God and their life, the lover of their soul. These intercessors did not do much of anything else; prayer is their life. They did not go to the movies, there were no theaters. They did not go for a manicure, there were no salons, get my drift. They were sold out and I knew it!

As it was time to leave, she walked us to the front door where we had entered; she opened the door, and then briskly shut the door. She looked at us with concern in her eyes, and said," We must use the back door!" Not realizing why, we just obeyed and followed her to exit the room. As we stepped outside of the back door, there was a steep incline, which was very rocky and uneven. Louann braced me as we made our way through the brush and up to the street. We looked back to see what the commotion was that we heard. There was yellow tape marking off areas in the street just in front of the doorway to this house of prayer. The Israeli police were surveying the area. We discovered that during our time of prayer, a young teenage boy, while riding his bicycle up the street, had thrown rocks at a police car. The police officer had jumped from his car and fatally gunned the boy down. Our dear sweet sister was trying to protect us from any fear or danger. We followed her swiftly up to a ledge, where we could view the other parts of the City of David. Gasping at what just transpired, I realized the heaviness of the times. Because of terrorism invading our world, especially since the twin towers were stroke in New York, safety is always an issue. More so it seems in the foreign land of which I am standing.

We lingered with her about thirty minutes more as she taught about the ruins that were near us. Then his precious end-time *Anna* held me in her arms and placed her time-worn hands on my shoulders and neck and said, "God has placed a *garland of grace* upon you and you will wear it the rest of your life." Words escape me as I try to write what I felt in that instant. I could have died and gone to heaven with complete satisfaction in my heart in fulfilling the will of God. This was heaven on earth to me.

After parting from her, we began to walk the streets of the city heading toward *Hezekiah's Tunnel* where we had planned to walk through the water flowing from the *Gihon Springs*.

This incredible tunnel is about forty-feet below ground level and around 135 feet long. The springs and tunnels allowed the natural water to flow out for the public and it ending up at the pool of *Siloam*. This water shaft was used by David and his men to enter and attack Jerusalem when it was occupied by the Jebusites.

> **"On that day David had said, 'Anyone who conquers the Jebusites will have to use the water shaft to reach those lame and blind who are David's enemies.' This is why they say the blind and lame will not enter the palace." (2 Samuel 5:8, NIV)**

Darla was taking us there so we could have the experience and the opportunity of a lifetime walking through the tunnels. She had told us the previous day that we had to each have a flashlight and wear certain clothing and rubber shoes in order to make the journey. Louann and I had found the attire we needed in the marketplace in the old city. After walking a short distance, we came to the entrance of the tunnels only to find out they had closed it off to the public for the day. We concluded it was due to the alarming situation of the death of the young boy. There was much scurrying about with the people of the city, and unfortunately experienced discomfort from the ominous presence which filled the atmosphere. We were hoping to end up at the pool of Siloam where the healing waters flow, but reluctantly found ourselves wanting to go back to the comfort and safety of our room.

"He answered and said, "A man that is called Jesus made clay and anointed my eyes, and said unto me, go to the pool of Siloam and wash," and I went and washed and I received sight." (John 9:11, KJV)

Chapter 13

~ *The Dead Sea* ~

"And the east border was the Salt Sea, even the even the end of Jordan. And their border in the north quarter was from the bay of the sea at the uttermost part of Jordan." (Joshua 15:5, KJV)

Originally, in Scripture, the *Dead Sea* was called the *Salt Sea*. Historically believed to be at least three million years old which is why some refer to it as the dinosaur sea. The Dead Sea is the lowest place on planet Earth, at 1385 feet below sea level. It is over a half a mile deep, fifty miles long, and eleven miles wide. It contains over 33% salt content. Obviously no fish or vegetation can exist, thus it was named, the Dead Sea. The *Jordan River* is the main tributary into the waters but no water flows out. Its salty waters contain enhancing minerals such as calcium, potassium. These elements are essential to human life, and magnesium in the water is like Epsom salt, which is frequently used today for soaking sore muscles.

Not only was this a refugee camp for King David, but later, the Dead Sea was considered the first health resort in the world started by King Herod. This hyper-saline water is eight times saltier than any other ocean of the world. The therapeutic qualities are remarkable, plus there's absolutely no pollution that can be found in the water. The weather is sunny and hot there year-round barely receiving any rainwater. We were eager to enjoy the natural buoyancy from the waters; which makes it impossible to swim or sink. If you ever make your way to the lowest place on earth, you will see hundreds of people simply floating in this land of the Bible phenomenon.

"Salt is good; but if the salt have lost his saltiness, wherewith will ye season it? Have salt in yourselves, and have peace with one another." (Mark 9:50, KJV)

This massive body of water spreads between the West Bank and Jordan. The Dead Sea spits up small pebbles and blocks of black substance which was used by the Egyptians for a balm for the mummification process. Because of the mineral content, the Sea water has a very bitter taste. The dense mud underfoot is full of healing proprieties. Learning all the amazing qualities that the Dead Sea possesses, of course we wanted to go and partake of this magnificent site.

Half way on the journey the air conditioner broke. It was well over one-hundred degrees and I thought Florida was hot! The team from the convocation, including Louann and I, tried to survive the heat; it was not easy, but possible.

We stopped at a small restaurant just before embarking on our journey to the Sea to have lunch and refresh ourselves. After our brief stay we all began to board the motor coach. As the driver turned the key, I quickly realized that Louann wasn't with me. The bus began to roll and I hurriedly stood up and screamed "My nurse-my nurse!" Everybody's attention turned toward me, for they had viewed the situation with my hands and knew that she was attending me on this journey with no hands. The bus came to a screeching halt.

We had driven about a three feet before seeing Louann walking up from the restaurant carrying two ice creams bars. Later, I chuckled under my breath at the alarming thought of our bus leaving her in the middle of the desert all because of an ice cream cone. It was an amusing sight being joined with a delightful treat this brutally hot day.

The third and best occurrence on our day trip to the Dead Sea, was meeting two new friends that were also a part of the convocation; they were from India and were mother and daughter. The mother's husband was a doctor in his village, who was very well-known, and the daughter was also a doctor herself but was feeling the call to establish a 24/7 prayer tower. After conversing with them, the daughter asked me if I would be willing to come to India and help her establish this prayer tower, to help train the people on intercessory prayer. I told her I would seek the Lord and get His council. Another astounding invitation at which I did not take lightly.

Walking down to the shore, preparing to enter the water, I pulled off my braces with my teeth and left them with my new doctor friend, who stayed on shore.

Soaking my arms in the hyper-saline, hyper-therapeutic waters, would speed up the process of healing on the actual surgery site on my skin.

Most people would wade out about waist deep, floating effortlessly, and would scoop down to the bottom and get to the mud under their feet and would pull it up and rub it on their bodies. Even on the postcards in the restaurant, we saw pictures of people covered completely in the mud. It has so much natural physical healing. Packs of this *mud* can sold and distributed all across the earth for its therapeutic element. Out in the water Louann began rubbing the mud all over my wrists as she began to pray for me. The more she prayed the louder she got, to the point that people around us were watching.

I raised my hands up toward the sky and began to praise the Lord for my healing, but not just on the skin, but all the way down through the bone and marrow area of my wrist.

I felt that God touched me in a phenomenal way. When I lowered my hands and opened my eyes, there was a man standing next to the Louann asking her to pray for his shoulder like she prayed for my arms. His shoulder was in excruciating pain. Louann scooped up the mud and smeared it on his shoulder as we both began to pray the healing power of Jesus. This man was most grateful as God begin to touch not only his shoulder but his heart as well. In the midst of all this, our young doctor friend heard the noise and joined us in prayer as I looked down at the surgery-strips I still had on, which were now *full* of mud; I asked her if she would deem it necessary to remove the bandages; honored to take care of this American girl, she nodded *yes* with a grin. We got out of the Sea and saw there was a fresh-water shower just a few feet from the shore. With my arms plunging underneath the water, she began to peel the strips off. After the cleansing of the mud and mire, we could plainly see the wounds were virtually closed up and looked much nicer than we expected. It just goes to show that God uses His creation to bring healing to His people. I was so grateful, that the *Great Physician* connected me with a doctor from India. Not just any doctor, but one who had a heart for prayer, one who loved Jesus with her entire life. It was a staggering thought that we stood in the middle of the desert, in the lowest part of the earth, the Dead Sea; yet the God of the Universe had connected our lives by using my physical brokenness. What a supernatural journey with no hands this has become. The luxury of this experience was indescribable. Only time will tell of my future in India.

"And the border shall go down to Jordan, and the goings out of it shall be at the Salt Sea; this shall be your land with the coast thereof round about." (Numbers 34:12, KJV)

Chapter 14

~ *Look Mom–No Hands!* ~

The time spent thus far here in the Land of the Bible has been life changing indeed. Learning the cultures, the people; we encountered lots of living, loving and laughing. The day God supernaturally used the person to pay my way here to Jerusalem, Louann shouted, "If God made a way for you to go, He will make a way for me too, even if I have to carry your bags! I am going with you!" Little did we know on that day that she *would* go and she *would* have to carry my bags? Along with having to spoon feed me, brush my teeth, bathe me, apply my makeup and dress me; thus my great adventure of travelling through Jerusalem with her hands and not mine. We watched the hand of God move so uniquely for her to be able to travel with me. Wonderfully I discovered that Louann was a Certified Nurse's Assistant and was very qualified to escort me into Israel. Plus she was adorned with a special grace from the Lord to care for me. I tell people the woman wears a permanent towel wrapped around her waist. She was in the truest since of the word, a godly servant to me. My wish was her command, she treated me like royalty. She made the most unpleasant circumstances seem joyous. She was polished and poised to be by my side literally day and night. Yet I must tell about the one and only time we were separated during our sixteen-day journey. She had bought a beautiful Jerusalem shofar and I wanted to surprise her and buy a case for it. So one night, after the service, we headed to the lobby of the Ramat Rachel Hotel where we were staying. Joining us were about 800 other people doing the same thing. In the mix of people I slipped away from her into the hotel gift shop where I had noticed a beautiful case the day before. As I bent my body down to view the article, I lost my balance. I could not allow myself to fall forward at the expense of more injury, so I just released myself to fall backward. Next thing I know I am flat on my back in the middle of the gift shop. I imagine I must have looked like a turtle on its back needing to be turned over.

> **"For if they fall, the one will lift him up his fellow: but woe to him that is alone when he falleth; for he hath not another to help him up." (Ecclesiastes 4:10, kjv)**

There were people walking all around me, yet, none-the-less, no one offered to help. Ninety-five percent of them could not speak English, maybe they assumed that since they couldn't talk to me that they could not help me either. After about five minutes of struggling, I somehow was able to roll over to my stomach and use my elbows to push up and reach a kneeling position. Only then I did manage to rise and go. So goes my journey through Jerusalem with no hands. Humiliated, I walked toward the elevator, pushed the button with my elbow and went to the sixth floor. I banged on our room door with my foot as Louann opened the door with this distraught look on her face. As I told her what happened through tears of laughter, she said, "One minute, just one minute alone and this happens!" You see you must understand that before we boarded the jumbo jet that day to leave the USA, my husband gave her *one* instruction, just *one*. He said, "Louann, whatever you do, don't let Janet fall." He then specifically told me to stay with her and not to stray.

He imaged the terrain would be rough in Jerusalem and he didn't want me to injure the surgery in any way. This is why it upset her that I had fallen.

Have you ever watched a young child learning to ride a bicycle, and think they can do it with no hands on the handle bars? They start off by screaming, *Look Mom no hands!* Then end up crashing. I guess that's what happened to me there in the lobby floor of the gift shop. What was I thinking when I purposefully left Louann in that massive crowd of people? One thing for sure I was *not* thinking; that I would crash after riding away.

There are two important directives I want to leave with you from this seemingly frivolous story. One, is not to revolve away from any plan that God puts in motion. We are commissioned to be a people under command, no matter how insignificant the order given may seem to be. Don't allow yourself to deviate in the slightest.

The other is to reach for Jesus when you fall; trusting Him to pick you up when life knocks you down or trips you up. Everything that concerns you, concerns Him. God will not only lift you up from any fallen state, He also will wipe the dust off and send you on your way again.

"The Eternal God is thy refuge and underneath are the Everlasting Arms." (Deuteronomy 33:27, KJV)

Chapter 15

~ *Jerusalem House of Prayer for All Nations* ~

—⟋⟍⟍◦◦⟋◦◦◦⟋◦◦⟋⟍—

"Even them will I bring to my holy mountain, and make them
joyful in my house of prayer; their burnt offerings and their
sacrifices shall be accepted upon mine altar; for my house shall
be called a house of prayer for all people." (Isaiah 56:7, KJV)

On the highest pinnacle of the *Mount of Olives*, the awe-inspiring
Jerusalem House of Prayer for All Nations gracefully stands. A magnificent
three-story edifice; with the first floor having rooms for classes and food
storage for the needy. The second floor having offices for their dedicated
staff, and the third floor having a large, round, prayer room with the
formation of a round, globe ceiling. Outside the prayer room are open
doorways to a full-circle balcony which puts all of Jerusalem wonderfully
on display. Twenty-four hours a day, seven days a week, people flow
through with intercession and worship. The shofars are skillfully blown
to heighten the spiritual awareness of God's presence and to invite Him
to come. There is constant prayer for the great harvest, the fullness of
intimacy with God, and the pertinent calling for Heaven and earth to
join together. There are 30 harpist who play skillfully and psalm in the
Hebrew language at certain intervals; such as the Global Day of Prayer.
The Jerusalem House of Prayer houses the *School of Prophetic Harp* and

a *School of Ministry* with the purpose of equipping people of prayer to become strong watchman on the walls of Jerusalem.

> **"I have set watchmen upon thy walls, O Jerusalem, which shall never hold their peace day nor night: ye that make mention of the Lord, keep not silence."** (Isaiah 62:6, KJV)

At least, 1,000 people from the convocation arrived on the grounds with anticipation of the day. Sitting on the lawn, there was a remarkable, dromedary camel. He was adorned with what looked like a hand-made saddle. Dear Louann chose to climb up on the back of it to further experience the authenticity of Jerusalem. Without thinking, I started to mount up as well; but soon realized I could not climb up and grip the saddle, briefly overlooking the fact that I could not use my hands.

Honestly, the things I could *not* do were minimal because Louann was the perfect pair of hands for me. She constantly went out of her way to subsidize my loss, but this was *one* thing she could not possibly do for me. Yet, as I watched her ride with sheer joy and laughter; I was fulfilled.

As the multitude quieted down; Tom Hess, the director, gave a most informative speech from a small balcony. The World Wide Watch that flows from here, purposefully channels the restoration of the *Tabernacle of David* to the ends of the earth, through the Twelve Gates of Jerusalem. One being the Jaffa Gate that I was called to.

> **After this I will return, and** *will build again the tabernacle which is fallen down; and I will build again the ruins thereof, and I will set it up.* **That the residue of men might seek after the Lord, and all the Gentiles, upon whom my name is called, saith the Lord, who doeth all these things."** (Acts 15:16–17, KJV) *emphasis mine*

Day and night, watchmen from many nations worship and pray in the twelve major languages of the world. The twelve languages are; Hebrew, Arabic, Hindi, Russian, English, Portuguese, Spanish, Chinese, German, French, Turkish and Indonesian.

They are watching and waiting for the Messiah and are preparing the way for the King of Glory; welcoming back the Messiah to the Mount of Olives.

> "Prepare the table, watch in the watchtower, eat, drink; arise, ye princes, and anoint the shield. For thus hath the Lord said unto me, Go, set a watchman, let him declare what he seeth." (Isaiah 21:5–6, KJV)

God is globally stationing watchman; which simply means, people of prayer, who observe and discern the times and the moves of the Spirit of God and guard the city with their intercession. Father God is building and re-building the house of prayer, in all nations, and in all people groups. It's time that unfamiliarity of the season we are living in is removed from Christian's minds, and also the limpness of a lethargic spirit is eliminated. Let's learn the design of Heaven and take our place in the restoration of prayer and worship in our own lives and the lives of others. I stated in chapter one, the vision of the World Wide Watch and its redemptive plans and purposes. Also, these certainties are to help escort people to their destinies in fulfilling the apostolic-prophetic call.

My heart found this *house* a place of great content. To know that constant prayer flows from here and accomplishes so much was inspiring. The scriptures declare that when Jesus returns to Earth, that His feet will touch the Mount of Olives. It is hard to fathom that we were standing on that very mountain. Magnificent and holy were the only words that escaped my lips. Being here and knowing Christ's return is imminent, made it become an even brighter reality.

> "On that day His feet will stand on the Mount of Olives, east of Jerusalem, and the Mount of Olives will be split in two from east to west, forming a great valley, with half of the mountain moving north and half moving south." (Zechariah 14:4, NIV)

Chapter 16

~ *Garden of Gethsemane* ~

During our exit from the Jerusalem House of Prayer, we were each handed a large palm branch that was at least six feet tall. The order of the day was to *relive* the moments of Christ. Over 1,000 radical Christians began chanting *hosannas* commencing our four miles down the Mount of Olives.

> "And when they had sung a hymn, they went out into the Mount of Olives." (Matthew 26:30, KJV)

> "On the next day much people that were come to the feast, when they heard that Jesus was coming to Jerusalem, took branches of palm trees, and went forth to meet him, and cried Hosanna: Blessed is the King of Israel that cometh in the name of the Lord." (John 12:12–13, KJV)

Our destination; the historical site of the ages, the *Garden of Gethsemane*. It was a laborious, yet exciting trek as we hiked down streets, marched around curves and wandered through villages. Passing a small local store, Louann and I stopped briefly to get a large bottle of fresh water for the journey. Outside the store we saw two little Jewish boys riding a donkey, they smiled and asked if we wanted a ride; Hmmmmm tempting…

We had walked miles in the scorching heat and we were parched. Louann placed the large water bottle between my braces so I could endlessly drink. Feelings of exhaustion were settling in on me. This peaked as being the most rigorous thing I had done since the surgery, my upper limbs were fine, but was my lower limbs were aching.

The final descent was so steep it caused us to almost run or we would fall flat on our faces. Have you ever seen a multitude of people trying to balance like this? It was a quite a scene. Certainly, Louann did not want me to fall and automatically put my hands out to brace myself, and neither did I. The incline became so hard to navigate that Louann placed her fingers through the belt loops of my pants to steady me for the duration. The view changed the further down the mountain we came. Nearing the base, we walked through a grove of olive trees. Many of them gnarled and hollow, yet still standing strong and able to bear fruit. These ancient trees thrive in the Mediterranean climate and can endure life for several thousand years. These stunning trees were embedded all around, giving us a delightful and welcomed shade.

"Then Jesus came with them to a place called Gethsemane and said to his disciples, sit here while I go and pray over there. And he took with him Peter and the two sons of that Zebedee and he began to be sorrowful and deeply distressed. Then he said to them, my soul is exceeding sorrowful, even to death." (Matthew 26:36–38, NKJV)

My eyes streamed with tears as I witnessed this consecrated site. I gasped waves of tender sorrow from the atmosphere itself. Then my eyes locked their gaze on the spot where it is told that Jesus prayed and surrendered His all. A tangible love gushed in and out from my wide-open heart. I was privileged to be here where Jesus, the Son of the Living God, prayed to give up his life for humanity. I was smitten with His undeniable love for mankind. I wanted to bow very low, and pray to the Father just as Jesus had done. Jesus was so submitted to the will of His Father that he yielded His total will, with full knowledge of what was ahead; the cross, the pain, and the crucifixion unto death.

> "For God so loved the world that He gave his only begotten son that whosoever believes in him should not perish but have everlasting life." (John 3:16, KJV)

Sobbing, I said to The Father that I wanted to submit my every moment, every hour, every day, and every year to Him. How could I not desire to become totally abandoned while kneeling in Jesus' place of total abandonment? An aura of grace was stimulating my heart as I pledged my allegiance to a place of surrender.

Jesus was born for destiny. His birth, death, burial, resurrection, and His return, are all in the plan of God. Yet in His humanity we hear him praying to the Father.

> "He went a little further and fell on His face, and prayed, saying, "Oh my Father, if it is possible, let this cup pass from Me; nevertheless, not as I will, but as You will." (Matthew 26:39, NKJV)

He was one-hundred percent man, and one-hundred percent God; that is why He prayed this prayer. Have you ever found yourself in your own Garden of Gethsemane? Having to make a decision of magnitude? When your flesh does not want to really submit, but in your heart, you know the best way is the Father's will? Sure, we all have at some point. I have gone to my own Gethsemane; my place of prayer, many times. Each time when I leave, I am changed because of a surrendered heart and His love flows over me fresh and new. From these experiences, I penned these words over thirty years ago.

Garden of Your Love
(Original song by Janet Penney 1983)

To be alone with you in my Gethsemane to feel
your presence in the garden of your love
When pressures of life they come and try to burden me
I run to Gethsemane to be alone with you
And the burdens fly away. When I spend my time with you

How I treasure this place, the garden of your love
To be alone with you, to hear your voice once more
The sweetest words have ever heard
To be alone with you in my Gethsemane
To feel your presence in the garden of your love
What a breath of fresh air your spirit brings to me
Sweep over my soul in the Garden of your love

The Garden of Gethsemane represents a place of great love and sacrifice.

"Greater love hath no man than this that a man lay down his life for his friends." (John 15:13, KJV)

This is monumentally true love in action.

"We love him, because he first loved us." (1 John 4:19, NKJV)

At times you may enter a Gethsemane moment, yet you do not exit any different than when you entered. If in leaving your place of earnest prayer you do not feel lighter, be still in your soul and surrender everything. It will never be easy, but it will be possible. Sometimes you may need to stay a little longer, and press a little harder, until you spiritually sweat some blood.

"And being agony he prayed more earnestly. Then his sweat became like great drops of blood falling down to the ground." (Luke 22:44, NKJV)

Chapter 17

~ *On This Street* ~

The *Via Dolorosa* is a street of two parts in Jerusalem which our Savior, Jesus Christ, walked on the way to His own crucifixion. After our Lord was condemned by *Pontius Pilate*, he began the 2,000 feet journey to die for humanity. The Via Dolorosa is also called, *the way of suffering, the way of sorrows, the way of grief or painful way.*

> "He is despised and rejected of men; a man of sorrows, and acquainted with grief; and we hid as it were our faces from him; he was despised, and we esteemed him not." (Isaiah 53:3, KJV)

On this street-

Has never walked anyone for the same cause that Jesus Christ did.

> "He was taken from prison and from judgment: and who shall declare his generation? For he was cut off of the land of the living: for the transgression of my people was he stricken. And he made his grave with the wicked and with the rich in his death; because he had done no violence, neither was any deceit in his mouth." (Isaiah 53:8–9, KJV)

On this street-

Jesus sauntered, understanding He was the Everlasting High priest after the order of Melchizedek, which gave Him authority to offer Himself as the spotless Lamb.

"The Lord hath sworn, and will not repent, thou art a priest forever after the order of Melchizedek." (Psalms 110:4, KJV)

On this street-

Jesus was prodded forward knowing He was replacing all the sacrificial offerings that ever were before Him.

"By that will we have been sanctified through the offering of the body of Jesus Christ once for all." (Hebrews 10:10, NKJV)

On this street-

Jesus yielded himself and took on the sin of the world.

"All we like sheep have gone astray; we have turned everyone to his own way; and the Lord hath laid on him the iniquity of us all." (Isaiah 53:6, KJV)

On this street-

Jesus freely became a sin offering for humanity.

"Yet it pleased the Lord to bruise him; he hath put him to grief: when thou shalt make his soul an offering for sin." (Isaiah 53:10, KJV)

On this street-

With all the pain, Jesus never complained.

"He was oppressed, and he was afflicted, yet he opened not his mouth: he has brought as a lamb to the slaughter, and as a sheep before her shearers is dumb, so he opened not his mouth." (Isaiah 53:7, NKJV)

On this street-
He paced and prayed for us through His suffering.

"Because he has poured out his soul unto death: and he was numbered with the transgressors; and he bare the sin of many, and made intercession for the transgressors." (Isaiah 53:12*b*, KJV)

On this street-
A completely innocent, human, man staggered under the weight of the cross.

"And as they came out, they found a man of Cyrene, Simon by name: him they compelled to bear his cross." (Matthew 27:32, KJV)

On this street-
The people were violently screaming for His death.

"But they cried out the more, saying, let him be crucified." (Matthew 27:23*b*, KJV)

On this street-
The Via Dolorosa that I am now walking on; the rhythm of my heart weeps, "I'm sorry Jesus they hurt you, I'm so sorry Jesus they were mean to you."

Chapter 18

~ *My Eyes Saw* ~

———⁓⁓⁓⁓⁓⁓———

"But God commanded his love toward us, in that, while we
were yet sinners, Christ died for us." (Romans 5:8, KJV)

As my eyes saw Golgotha, they clenched tight straining to view the
gruesome place of our Savior's death. The uniquely formed rocks were
forcefully displaying the shape of a skull. I envisioned Christ hanging
there on a cross, bleeding and dying for me.

"And he bearing his cross went out to a place called the
Place of the Skull, which is in Hebrew, Golgotha, where
they crucified Him, and two others with Him, one on either
side, and Jesus in the center." (John 19:17-18, NKJV)

By the time I reached this place on my journey, my spirit was totally
transformed. This was real, He died for me! Jesus' death was factual
and genuine. The familiar words on the pages of the Bible were now
flourishing in the caverns of my soul.

"Then they took the body of Jesus and wound it in linen
clothes with the spices, as the manner of the Jews is to
bury. Now in the place where he was crucified there
was a garden; and in the garden a new tomb in which
no one had yet been laid." (John 19:40–41, NIV)

After His crucifixion, Jesus laid in the grave for three days. But on the third day he rose from the dead.

> "So they both ran together and the other disciple outran Peter and came to the tomb first. And he, stooping down and looking in, saw the linen clothes lying there; yet he did not go in. Then Simon Peter came, following him, and went into the tomb. And he saw the clothes lying there and the handkerchief that had been about his head, not lying with the linen clothes, but folded together in a place by itself." (John 20:4–7, NKJV)

Walking only a few feet, my eyes saw the tomb where they laid His body. Travel with me to the same spot, seeing with your eyes, what Mary Magdalene, Simon Peter, and the beloved disciple saw that first Easter morning.

> "Then the other disciple, who came to the tomb first, went in also; and he saw and believed. For as yet they did not know the scripture that He must rise again from the dead." (John 20: 8–9, NKJV)

Can you imagine how I am feeling? Can you put yourself in the moment with me? Close your eyes and imagine looking in the tomb, the empty tomb, and seeing the place where Jesus Christ once laid. Visualize yourself walking inside, as they did, and I am doing now. How are you feeling? What are your thoughts? All that would come from my lips were, "Thank you Jesus for dying for me, I love you, I love you Jesus."

The tomb has two small chambers, one was called the *preparation* chamber where the body was prepared with spices. The other is the *burial* chamber where the body was placed to perpetually lay. Every other corpse in the world was meant to be there perpetually, but the *only One ever* who did not stay was Jesus! This is what sets Him apart from all other gods and all other forms of religion. All I can do is weep. Yet, I am not only weeping because Jesus died, I am weeping because he is *not* here! Rejoicing with tears of joy that Jesus is alive and well!

Remarkably, this particular tomb was brand new when our Lord was placed here; I witnessed marks of chiseling where it was possibly under construction when Joseph of Arimathea gave it to the disciples for Jesus.

> **"When even was come, there came a rich man of Arimathea, named Joseph, who also himself was Jesus's disciple: he went to Pilate, and begged the body of Jesus. Then Pilate commanded the body to be delivered. And when Joseph had taken the body, he wrapped it in a clean linen cloth, and laid it *in his own new tomb*, which he had hewed out in the rock: and he rolled a great stone to the door of the scepter and departed."** (Matthew 27:57-60, KJV) *emphasis mine*

Understand, I am not standing at the tomb of *Elvis Presley*, *Buddha* or *Mohammed*, or any of these other so-called idols. I am standing inside the *empty tomb* of Jesus Christ the Son of God, the Son of Man! I am seeing with my own eyes this infallible truth that even death could not hold him!

My eyes saw the 4,000 pound door which had a small channel underneath it. This channel was used to roll the door open; this in itself was a site to behold. Now standing just outside the tomb, my heart was singing," Resurrection power lives within my soul; resurrection power comes and makes me whole". My body was gently trembling with that same power, the resurrection power which can cause human flesh to tremble.

> **"Jesus said to her, I am the resurrection and the life: he who believes in me, though he may die, he shall live."** (John 11:25a, NKJV)

Reading about it, hearing sermons about it, and even seeing pictures and movies do not give justice to seeing it with your own eyes. As I stated before, the majority of people will never be afforded the privilege of coming to Israel. This is the reason that I am writing meticulously, giving my thoughts, feelings and emotions, with the intent, that you, the reader, can have your spirit and soul illuminated to these undeniable truths.

> "For God so loved the world that He gave his only begotten son that whosoever believes in him should not perish but have everlasting life." (John 3:16, KJV)

We all were created with a God-shaped vacuum inside us. There is nothing else in this life that can fill that void. No relationship, no drug, no alcohol, no job, absolutely nothing or no one has the capability to complete you. That aching, that gnawing, that I once had has left me since I made Jesus my Lord and Savior. It is never too late for the *Truth* that will completely set you free from sin.

Lord means boss or owner, He doesn't want to be an accessory in your life, neither does He want something from you, He just wants *you*. What are you going to do with your one and only life?

> "Then you will call upon me, and go and pray unto me, and I will listen to you. And you will seek me, and find me, when ye search for me with all your heart." (Jeremiah 29:12–13, KJV)

If you have not invited Jesus into your life, what are you waiting for? Today is the day of salvation.

> "For he says, 'in the time of favor I have heard you, and in the day of salvation I have heard you.' I tell you now is the time of God's favor, now is the time of salvation." (2 Corinthians 6:2, NIV)

It has been said for centuries that there is no time like the present, and how definite are these words for us today.

> "That if you will confess with your mouth the Lord Jesus, and believe in your heart that God raised him from the dead, you will be saved. For with the heart one believes unto righteousness, and with the mouth confession is made into salvation." (Romans 10:9–10, NKJV)

None of us have the promise of tomorrow.

> "Whereas you do not know what will happen tomorrow. For what is your life? It is even a vapor that appears for a little time and then vanishes away." (James 4:14, NKJV)

Please take this weighty Bible verses to heart today, don't waste another minute, ask Jesus to become your Savior and Lord. It is just that simple. All He wants is for you to invite Him and He will come. Then you can experience true life, joy, and peace. These attributes possess the strength to carry you through each day no matter how heavy your burdens may be. There will be times when you may fall under the weight of your troubles; God will be faithful and send a *Simon* to you, someone to be at your side to help carry your cross. Remember what I said earlier, that Jesus is our example, and if the Father did it for His Son, then He will do it for you. We are made *one* in Him.

> "I do not pray for these alone, but also for those who will believe in me through their word. That they all may be one; as you father are in me and I am in you; that they also may be one in us, that the world may know that you sent me." (John 17: 20–21, NKJV)

Chapter 19

~ *Upper Room* ~

"He told them, 'This is what is written: the Messiah will
suffer and rise from the dead on the third day, and forgiveness
for the repentance of sins will be preached in his name to
all nations, beginning at Jerusalem. You are witnesses of
these things. I am going to send you what my Father has
promised; but stay in the city until you have been clothed
with power from on high.'" (John 26:46–49, NIV)

It's very plainly written here that Jesus was ascending to the Father
in Heaven, but that He was sending back to earth a promise from the
Father; His Holy Spirit. He knew that to overcome life situations we
would have to have power living within.

"And when they were come in they went up into an upper
room, where abode both Peter, and James, and John, and
Andrew, Philip, and Thomas, Bartholomew, and Matthew,
James the son of Alpheus, and Simon Zelotes, and Judas
the brother of James. These all continued with one accord
in prayer and supplication, with the women, and Mary the
mother of Jesus, and his brethren." (Acts 1:13–14, KJV)

When my feet stepped inside the historical *Upper Room* in Jerusalem,
I was drenched with the presence of the Holy Spirit. Being much smaller

than I had visualized, with a small platform, along with its low ceilings and tiny windows. Immediately I found a private corner and fell to my knees in honor of God. I began to pray in my heavenly language which surged forth like a powerful water fountain. The intensity increased; seemingly, I was experiencing a similar touch like the disciples had on the day the gift of the Holy Ghost was first given; The Day of Pentecost. How humbled was I to stand in the room where the Father first send His Holy Spirit to the world. After ten to fifteen minutes had passed, I looked up and noticed I had become a spectacle to some bystanders, but it mattered not. It could not be denied, His *Gift* had been given to me and I had received it.

"And when the day of Pentecost was fully come, they were all with one accord in one place. And suddenly there came a sound from heaven as of a rushing mighty wind, and it filled all the house where they were sitting. And there appeared unto them cloven tongues like as of fire, and it sat upon each of them. And they were all filled with the Holy Ghost, and began to speak with other tongues, as the Spirit gave them utterance." (Acts 2:1-4, KJV)

I realize this subject is very controversial, yet I speak from my own personal experience. I know *whose* I am. I have been bought with the price of the blood of Jesus. God has sent His Spirit to the earth, and I have received Him into my life. I too have been endued with power from on high, just like the Scripture has spoken. The divine Holy Spirit keeps me, guides me, and comforts me. He also teaches by instructing me in my daily walk. Some Christians do not agree with the speaking of unknown tongues after they receive Christ. Yet I cannot think of how a person could have an ice cube in their mouth and say," I want the cube of ice, but I do not want any water." They are one in the same, God the Father, God the Son, and God the Holy Spirit.

He is a gift and I treasure, honor, and esteem Him with every fiber of my being. It's Him who makes me live, love and laugh in this life. It's His countenance on my face, His shimmer in my eyes, His words in my speech. It's the Holy Spirit who helps me to live a life of prayer, who gives me strength to do the impossible. Without Him, the authenticity of who I am would not exist.

Chapter 20

~ *Quantum Leap or Casual Stance* ~

Years ago there was a popular song called *Casual Christian*. It went like this:

> *I don't want to be, I don't want to be a casual Christian. I don't want to live; I don't want to live a lukewarm life. I want to light up the night, be a living sacrifice. I don't want to live a casual Christian life.**

These words have followed me around since the day I first heard them. One night back home in America, as I lay in bed praying for a particular friend, the word *quantum* floated up from my spirit. I began to pray the word over my friend, that she would take quantum leaps in her life. I began to desire the same for myself and my loved ones as well. Upon awakening the next morning the word was still there.

Quantum (n) - gross quantity, mass volume, bulk.

Reflectively, a seed was planted within me. While watching a Christian television program recently, there was a guest author heralding his new book; spontaneously out of my mouth came, "I want to be on that show, I want to sit in that chair and share my new book!" About that time my husband walked in the room and I said, "You see that show?" "Yes, You want to be on it right?" he replied. Well in the mouth of two or three witnesses let every word be established.

> "But if he will not hear, take with you one or two more,
> that by the mouth of two or three witnesses every word
> may be established." (Matthew 18:16, NKJV)

That would be another quantum leap for me. My heart began to sing that familiar song. Yet again, I delved into the familiar Webster's Dictionary for the meaning of the other words in the song.

Casual (adj)-Feeling of showing little concern, nonchalant, lack of high degree, of interest or devotion. Done without serious intent or commitment. Occurring by chance, without regularity. Met on with occasion, superficial.

Upon unearthing this meaning I surely *did not* want to be a casual Christian! I want my life to leave a wake of goodness long after I am gone; a godly legacy.

On my ascent into Jerusalem after the divine invitation had come to me, I realized that my life had taken its first real quantum leap in the spirit.

I went from standing on the wall in a very small house of prayer, to singing prophetically over Jerusalem and standing shoulder to shoulder with heads of nations.

My soul can no longer be satisfied with a meager or mundane Christian walk. I want to light up the night, be a living sacrifice. Do you? Do you want to make a difference in your world? We all have greatness inside us placed there by our Creator. We must strive to fulfill our destiny and reach our greatest potential, whatever that may look like. Pushing, pressing, pursuing to achieve our absolute best is a powerful way to spiritual satisfaction. Giving our lives away to bear His Name only glorifies Him more. Is there anything I ask, of greater value in this life? No longer can we have a *Que sera, sera- whatever will be, will be*, attitude. Rather, decide to make a difference, choose to go the distance. We can't leave up to Him, what He left up to us. Decisions determine direction and direction determines destination or *destiny*.

About a week and a half had passed and strength steadily had been returning to my limbs. One evening, I had a little alone time in our room. I decided to take a shower by myself for the first time since the accident. Yet living again the title of this book, I couldn't handle the weight of the blow dryer; so I walked through the open French doors and onto our balcony. The plan was to set in a chair and let the breeze of Israel dry my hair. As I sat there viewing the city, I felt the Holy Spirit blowing through my very existence. I sensed the Light of Heaven on my balcony. Opening my mouth I began to sing prophetically over Jerusalem from the words of Psalms 125:2

"As the mountains are round about Jerusalem, so the Lord is round about His people from henceforth even forever."

And also from the words of Psalms 147:2-3

"The Lord doth build up Jerusalem: he gathers it together. The outcasts of Israel, he healeth the broken in heart, and bind us up their wounds."

I was singing these verses repetitively, declaring that Jerusalem is the apple of His eye, and calling the people forth from this great city, the City of the Great King. I want to always light up the night, the darkness, anyway I possibly can. We can do extraordinary things in the most informal manner, or the most informal things in the most extraordinary manner.

Chapter 21

~ *Ten Days of Awe* ~

As the convocation came to a close, arriving on *Rosh Hashanah* and ending on *Yom Kippor*, we had completed the *Ten Days of Awe*; *Yamin Noriam*, which actually means *Days of Repentance*. These days were designed as a time of introspection, a time to seek reconciliation between God and man. I don't claim to be a savant concerning the beautiful Jewish traditions that are so vast. Discussing them all would be like trying to point out a favorite piece of candy in a large gourmet candy store, or a favorite book in the largest library containing thousands of volumes. Jewish traditions had not been my purpose at all in writing this book. Although, I have tried to define the marvelous paradigm shift that has taken place inside me. Changing not only who *He is*, but also, who *I am*. My aspiration in writing this book was the desire to adorn your thoughts with the realities of the only Supreme Being, the only True Deity.

> "Which in his times he shall shew, who is the blessed and only Potentate, the King of Kings, and Lord of Lords." (1 Timothy 6:15, KJV)

Louann and I came into Jerusalem celebrating Israel's New Year/ Rosh Hashanah with thousands of people from every nation of the world. We spent time praying during the special services and in several individual HOP. Now, almost two weeks later, we were about to leave Jerusalem the morning after *Yom Kippor*.

Late on one of the final nights, I was sleeping because I partook in an early morning watch that day. Louann was in the large convocation auditorium doing a night watch. She was called on the platform to pray for the United States; being the only American present. Later, entering the hotel room ecstatically, she awakened me with bubbling laughter trying to tell me what happened. She spoke of how she felt so honored to be the *one person* to stand in the gap that night for our country. The joy echoing from her made my heart sing! Not only had Louann Moore been *my hands*, she now had become *my mouth*! In reality, not just mine alone, but a voice in the earth which all the intercessors could follow. We are the temple, the body, in which prayer should be constantly flowing. We are a *house of prayer*.

Preparing to leave the Ramet Rachel Hotel after most of our things were packed; we took a little stroll down the hallways to say good-bye to our treasured friends. Then we went down to the lobby and noticed a sign in front of the hotel restaurant which read: *Saturday-Closed due to fasting in observance to Yom Kippor*. Now that's a sign you will never see where I come from, it was wonderful! Yom Kippor, the *Day of Atonement*, which is referred to as the *High Holy Day*, or the holiest day of the year, is a day when everyone fasts. No open restaurants, no businesses in operation, no busses running, even the television stations were shut down. This final day of the Ten Days of Awe concluded with people humbling themselves with repentance before the Messiah; Yeshua. It is a *Sabbath of Sabbaths*. Privileged to be a part of this life-changing day; we bowed our hearts low in solemnness with fasting and prayer.

Walking out on the balcony of our hotel room, I glanced across the city. No one in the streets, no moving cars; it was similar to a ghost town in a western movie. How tremendous to view an entire region in such a place of stillness and reverence.

The next day was Sunday and Louann and I were checking out of our hotel. The lobby was rustling with employees. To the Jewish, this was their Monday, yet it seemed odd to me as a Westerner. Generally speaking, Christians allude to the fact that Sunday is our day of rest; yet not calling it the Sabbath, but rather, the Lord's Day or just simply Sunday. I researched and found that around the year 321, the Roman

Catholics changed the days even though it is not authorized in the Bible to do.

It takes thirty days to make a discipline, sixty days a habit, and ninety days, a lifestyle. Would to God that people of every nation would take a day, a month, or better yet, a *lifetime* of humbling themselves before God? The world would be a better place, and the purity of Jesus in our lives would be more visible. There is more to be *gained* in Christ than to be *lost* in Judaism.

For me, walking in these last ten days represents more of a lifestyle than just a few days; each day is the Lord's Day. I will stand in *awe* the rest of my life as I serve Jesus Christ.

Chapter 22

~ *Lost in the Wilderness* ~

Leaving the convocation, and knowing my deepest heart's desire; Ruth, Darla, Louann, and I rented a car and heading off on the six-hour drive to the Sea of Galilee, just so I could swim in its waters. Between the two of them living in Israel, they knew the roads and were familiar with the checkpoints that we must go through, etc. On the way there we stopped where Jesus gave the great *Sermon on the Mount*, commonly called the *Mount of Beatitudes*. Just the scenery alone was breathtaking, and the atmosphere seemed sacred. Being able to place my feet on the same ground that Christ did thousands of years ago, a place where He ministered to the multitudes was awe-inspiring. We spread a small blanket on the ground and pulled out our picnic lunch. No, it was not two fish and five loaves.

A soft breeze blew across the top of the mountain as the four of us took our places on the ground to break bread together. Many people were meandering around us as they were taking pictures, you could see the fascination on their faces and hear it in their conversations. Just then a tour bus drove up and the people began to unload. My eyes landed on one particular person, she was a beautiful young lady, with her wispy blonde hair blowing in the wind. She had been a dancer at the convocation in Jerusalem. I recalled her petite frame gracefully flowing with the worship music; she was a vision of loveliness in the eyes of God and man. Shimmering with the pure the light of God, with His countenance on her face. I motioned for her to come and set with us on the blanket and she gladly accepted. She introduced herself as *Evi*, and when she spoke I recognized an accent. I asked her where she had come from to be a part of the convocation. Smiling she said, "Budapest, Hungary". She spoke of her love for dancing, and of her place of worship back home in Budapest. After we finished our small meal, using my teeth I began to pull my braces off to get a little relief from the heat. Evi swiftly stopped me and began to pull them off herself. Delicately she held my wounded limbs in her hands and began to tenderly massage my arms, hands and fingers. She spoke of her training to become a physical therapist of some sort. What needed relief she brought to me that day. This was my second God-ordained therapy here in Israel. This simple act of kindness not only brought a measure of healing, it had given me a glance into the heart of God and the country of Hungary; an indescribable moment indeed. As we sat there together, the possible sight were one of the greatest miracles happened; where Jesus fed the 5,000 with two fishes and five loaves, I received my own *small miracle*. In addition, God had given me a sweet divine connection with one of His precious worshippers.

"And he commanded the multitude to sit down on the grass, and took the five loaves, and the two fishes, and looking up to heaven, he blessed, and brake, and gave the loaves to his disciples, and the disciples to the multitude. And they did all eat, and were filled: and they took up the fragments that remained twelve baskets full. And they that had eaten were about five thousand men, beside women and children." (Matthew 14:19-21. KJV)

Shortly thereafter, Ruth, Darla, Louann and I headed toward Tiberius. After driving just a few hours we found ourselves near *Jericho* in the *Judean Wilderness*. I mean it was a real wilderness! It looked like we were on the moon. Miles and miles of wasteland with sand dunes, hills, and mountains; what a picture of emptiness and loneliness. Often, we would see small man-made homes which reminded me of people that would be sojourning in the Bible. There might be a few goats there as well. I wondered how they had water for the animals and themselves since they were so far removed from everything and everyone. I tried to imagine what Jesus must have experienced when He spent forty days and nights fasting and praying here.

> **"Then was Jesus led up of the Spirit into the wilderness to be tempted of the devil. And when he had fasted forty days and forty nights, he was afterward a hungered."** (Matthew 4:1–2, KJV)

The hour was late and darkness was falling across the mountains of the lonely wilderness. Ruth, who was driving, was having a few doubts that we were heading in the right direction. Imagine driving in the desert with no billboards, and no signs to guide your way. There were no city lights and we saw no other cars on the road. I didn't even want to imagine what would happen if we had car trouble. I guess we would have to camp out. Hmmm, have you ever been in such a place in your own life? Maybe you felt lost in a barren place within your soul. You were so alone, and maybe the vehicle of your life was broken down and you were not moving in the things of God. You found yourself reluctantly having to camp out in a place you did not desire. As you survey the situation, your heart begins to feel dry because there is no flow of Living Water from the throne of Heaven, and no fresh manna. Sure, all of us have been there at some point in our lives. Even Jesus, the Son of Man, was weary and thirsty after being in Judaea.

> **"Now Jacob's well was there.** *Jesus therefore, being wearied with his journey,* **sat thus on the well: and it was about the sixth hour. There cometh a woman of Samaria to draw water:** *Jesus said unto her, 'Give me to drink.'"* **(Matthew 4:6–7, KJV)** *emphasis mine*

It is in these dry and desert times we have to lean on the breast of Jesus. Trusting is there in full assurance that He will satisfy us once again. Your faith must come into action at this point. Believing in what you cannot see or feel. In our walk with God, we don't always *feel* His presence. And that's okay, because feelings are inconsistent. The inner strength that comes through deeply embedded joy will carry you. Allow your faith and joy to dominate the situation. Keep your focus clear, and don't look to the left or right.

You may not always look where you are going,
but you will always go where you are looking.

Keep your gaze locked on Jesus and He will lead you up and out of your wilderness and into His joyous presence where the Living Water flows freely.

> "Behold, God is my salvation; I will trust, and not be afraid: for the Lord Jehovah is my strength and my song; he also is become my salvation. Therefore with joy shall you draw waters out of the wells of salvation." (Isaiah 12:2–3, KJV)

> "The joy of the Lord is your strength." (Nehemiah 8:10, KJV)

As the hours went by groping in this vast darkness, we finally saw a small light in the distance. As we approached, we realized it was a checkpoint that we were required to stop at. The Israeli military talked to Ruth in the Hebrew dialect, so I didn't know what was being said. I was praying under my breath because the conversation seemed a little heated to me. Ruth then pointed to me and Louann in the backseat and said, "They are Americans." We were asked to show our passports. She asked the man for directions to Galilee, and he said to keep going straight until we come to a small turn off road on the right. Leaving the checkpoint we all felt relieved, we began to sing and laugh and rejoice that we were now headed in the right direction. Our car was going about sixty miles an hour in the black of night, when suddenly, right before us was a roadblock across the entire road. We all screamed and shut our eyes, preparing for what was about to happen. In the half a second we had our eyes closed, we had crossed over to the other side of the roadblock and never felt a thing! The crash into the roadblock that we all knew was imminent, never occurred! We began screaming with delight and belly-laughing unto tears. As we looked behind us, the roadblock had not even been *touched*! The thickness of the glory of God flooded in our car. It was as if angels squeezed our car and made it smaller or they moved the roadblocks... either way it was a supernatural encounter, one that I will *never* forget!

Chapter 23

~ *Swimming in the Sea of Galilee* ~

It was about 10:00 p.m. as we miraculously made our way to Galilee and found our hotel. As my three friends were obtaining the key and retrieving the luggage, I waited on the second floor just outside our hotel room. Sometimes I felt bad because I literally could do nothing to help, not even open a door. At this point the pain in my wrists was decreasing; still I had no strength and no grip. While standing at the door alone, I could not see the water, but there was water leaking from my eyes. This was paramount of my personal desires; to swim in the Sea which is the *harp of God*.

Turning my eyes toward a small bush beside the door, I noticed a beautiful tiny bird that was singing sweetly. My heart felt like his, for it was singing sweetly as well. The deeper I observed this tiny bird, I noticed another bird of the same kind sitting near him, then another and another. Surprised, I counted twenty-four impressive little birds singing praises to the Lord. Instantly I thought of the book of Revelation and the twenty-four elders.

"And when those beasts give glory and honor and thanks to Him that sat on the throne, who liveth forever and ever, *the four and twenty elders fall down before Him that sat on the throne,* **and worship Him that lives forever and ever, and cast there crowns before the throne, saying thou art worthy oh Lord to receive glory and honor and power; for Thou hast created all things, and for Thy pleasure they are and were created.**" (Revelation 4:9–11, KJV) *emphasis mine*

Of late, I studied the book of Revelation for an entire year, in that year my soul was illuminated with *Who* He is. He is transcendent, being infinitely superior to everything that is created and is *wholly other than* all that exists. The twenty-four elders represents the body of Christ; you and I. With that being said, the Lord used this scenario to touch me in a most intimate way. My mind scrabbled to put the pieces together; the Sea, the birds, the sounds of worship, the music of Heaven, the pleasure of this moment; the harp of God!

If I had been helping the others get our luggage I would have missed the precious interval with my Creator. This definitely was one of the *few* times I was grateful to be on this journey with no hands.

I am learning more with the passing of each day that God is extremely into the details of our lives. The previous verse declares He made all things for His pleasure, stop and think about that for a minute. If we could peer though God's eyes and see the beauty that He sees; life would be pleasant. He is the Rose of Sharon releasing the scent of heaven, the Lily of the Valley awesomely displaying His beauty, the Voice of many waters calling forth His army and singing over us His love songs. At the same time, our Great High Priest that is touched with the feelings of our infirmities. What an awesome God!

"In that day it shall be said to Jerusalem, Fear thou not: and to Zion, Let not thy hands be slack. The Lord thy God in the midst of thee is mighty; he will save, he will rejoice over thee with joy; he will rest in his love, he will joy over thee with singing" (Zephaniah 3:16–17, KJV).

My hands are figuratively slack, yet I am very busy working for the cause of Christ. On this journey I have only used my hands to play the Harp of God. He is rejoicing over me as this scripture declares. As I sing unto the Lord my God, He sings back. What a marvelous exchange!

Our hotel room had two sets of bunk beds. I don't ever recall a hotel in America with bunk beds, anyway, it was perfect for the four of us to get a good night's sleep. For on the morrow we were heading down to the Sea, my precious, long awaited, Sea of Galilee.

Before dawn I heard the hotel door shut. I sat up and looked around the room to discover that Louann was gone. I then drifted off into a very light slumber. Then I heard the door again, she had returned and came to me and whispered, "Janet, get up. You've got to see it! The sun is almost up, let's share it together." I quietly got up and the two of us walked down to capture the sun rising on the Sea. On our way to the shore, I was transfixed by a huge, gorgeous, willow tree about one-hundred yards from the water. Its branches were blowing in the wind of the new day's arrival. I raised my hands and let my fingers dance along the soft branches. For those of you who don't know me, the willow tree is very significant to me.

> **"I will pour my spirit upon thy seed, and my blessing upon thy offspring:** *And they shall spring up as among the grass, as willows by the water courses.* **One shall say, I am the Lord's; and another shall call himself by the name of Jacob; and another shall subscribe with his hands unto the Lord, and surname himself by the name of Israel."** (Isaiah 44:3b–5, KJV) *emphasis mine*

Years ago I took these verses and put Mitchell, Charity and Leah's names in the place of the three people being referred to. Then I took my three small children to the local library and we did a study on the willow tree. Since I was homeschooling at the time, I had them each to write a paper about the tree. We discovered together that there are over 1000 types of willow trees. We learned that the roots of the tree will grow extremely long in search for a drink; they require lots and lots of water. They will even wrap their roots around water pipes. Desperate for life-giving liquid, just like we, as Christians should be for Jesus; the Living Water. I taught my children that they must go to any length to wrap themselves around the water that flows from heaven. You cannot survive without Him. From that day to this I still refer to my children as *willows*. I made up this catchy little song to sing over them.

Willows by the water courses, so beautiful to see
Willows by the water courses, such a handsome tree

Weeping willows water raised from a small sapling
Willows by the water courses they belong to God and me
They stand so strong and tall
And they will never fall
Their roots they grow so deep
As Your face Lord we seek
Willows by the water courses mean so, so much to me

What a sweet diversion. I'm running my fingers through the branches of this resplendent tree, having this precious moment with the Branch that I grow from, the Vine that I cling to. God knows how vibrantly connected I am to my family, and that our love runs deep. What a sweet reminder of my husband our children, who, by the way, are now married and have given us six grandchildren, joyfully representing many more willows. It was like they were standing there with me about to take in the moment I had been longing for. He is the God of the families.

~~~~~~

"At the same time, saith the Lord, will I be the
God of all the families of Israel, and they shall
be my people." (Jeremiah 31:1, kjv)

~~~~~~

The sun was now barely peeking over the mountains in its brilliant red and orange color, ahhh, it was rapturous!

~~~~~~

"After these things Jesus went over the sea of Galilee,
which is the sea of Tiberias." (John 6:1, kjv)

~~~~~~

I endeavored to take in this blissful moment. I may not pass this way again, so I was relishing every single breath, memorizing every single view, embracing each inspiring second. As my toes touched the tip of the water, I wept. Looking at the majestic mountains beside the sea, the probable area where he gave the Beatitudes, I began to visualize Jesus Christ, the Son of God, actually walking this shore, swimming in this water, better yet *walking on the water!*

Inch my inch, I began to ease my way into the water, I did not want to rush through this segment of time that seemed like a dream. The radiance of the morning sun was beaming over the beautiful mountain range. I used my teeth to take off my wrist braces, walked back to the shore, dropped them there on the sand, and walked back out into the water about waist deep.

Our friends, Ruth and Darla, met us about that time and walked out to where we were standing and we seized the moment, lavishing in the Love of God. It was in Louann's heart to baptize me in the Sea of Galilee, knowing that my greatest desire was to receive all that God had for me in this extraordinary place. The three of them stood around me quoting the scriptures then began to pray as I raised my hands. My heart was leaping with anticipation as they gingerly laid me back into the water, careful not to bring any harm, for it was the first time I had done anything with my braces off. When I came up out of the water I screamed the top of my voice "He is so faithful! He is so faithful!"

In the same manner that my spirit was leaping, my body dove head first into the water! I swam vivaciously and came up laughing in the Holy Ghost; the joy of the Lord washing over my entire being. This was the most exhilarating moment of my entire journey! I guess I looked like a dolphin, jumping in the water and going under and doing flips and laughing with great glee. For one brief moment, I thought about the night that I had broken my wrist at the altar and I cried, "I must go to Israel, I've got to swim in the Sea of Galilee." It looked impossible in that moment, but here I am in the new moment that God had ordained, the dream in my heart had come true! The devil had been defeated in my life. The more I thought about this, the more I laughed and swam and flipped like a beautiful fish in the ocean. It was invigorating!!!! When I slowed down enough, I saw Louann out of the corner of my eye, she was trying to catch up with me, wanting to keep me safe and unharmed. Certain by the way I was swinging around my arms that I was going to injure myself. Yet, I was moving so swiftly that she could not catch or contain me! Nothing or no one could stop this holy volcanic eruption from deep within my being. There was a rope along the water for the purpose of safety so we would not go out too deep.

I swam toward the rope, went under the rope on purpose and swam a few feet out into the deep water and screamed with all my might, "I cannot be contained!"

These are the same words I proclaimed the day I was being wheeled out of the hospital after my wrist surgery. The pain I felt that day when my one finger hit the ivory key was now completely gone.

In that moment, I felt I could do anything or go anywhere. It was as if the Holy Spirit was literally carrying me, flipping me, dipping me in and out of the water as I yielded myself completely to Him. All the pain from the past few weeks seemed as nothing. This joy of destiny was so great that I am having a very hard time putting it into words. Prophecy was fulfilled that day over me. For out of my own mouth, I had declared that I *would* swim in the Sea of Galilee that I would swim in the very Harp of God. Sincerely, with God in me and on me-I cannot be contained from doing anything He designs for me to do. For I am a harp, I am a song, I am music! Just as music can cross any language bearer, I feel I have crossed over into the language of Heaven; I will never be the same again.

Chapter 24

~ *Bridal Chamber~*

After our unforgettable swim in the Sea of Galilee, Louann and I had a few days before our return flight to the United States. Darla managed to arrange for her, Louann, and I, to stay in a two-bedroom apartment on the property of the Jerusalem House of Prayer, free of charge. As we drove up the Mount of Olives and into the driveway of the apartment building; we were shocked to see that the only passage to the front door was up an extremely steep staircase made of jagged rocks. Louann took our luggage out of the trunk of the car as we both stared crazily and shared in a moment of silent meditation. We were not being spiritual at all, just gasping at the thought of her and Darla hauling our heavy suitcases up the rugged walkway. I don't think I had wished to have use of my hands more than at this time.

Once inside, Louann sprawled out on the floor in either relief, or pain; I honestly couldn't tell. We went to bed early and in the stillness of the night we could hear the prayer and worship ascending from the Jerusalem House of Prayer.

Rising early the next morning, Darla led us up a rocky path from the porch of the apartment. The path led us to the back of the Jerusalem House of Prayer. If that wasn't interesting enough; as we approached the building there was a cement wall about six feet high in which there was *no* gate. Darla expressed that to walk down the apartments rock stairway, and out into the street, then up the house of prayer's even steeper driveway, would be harder still. We couldn't help to laugh because Darla called this the *better* way. There was an old ladder hanging on the cement wall which people often used. I looked at Darla and Louann and said, "How can I climb this ladder, I can't grip at all?" They both said at the same time, "We will help you." I will leave the rest up to your imagination, but I did semi-successfully make it over the wall. Let me advise you to never try to climb a ladder without use of your hands! Never!

Ruth was already in the house of prayer, fulfilling her duties. Once she was finished, we followed her up a small stairwell and into a beautiful *white* room. When I say white, I mean white. The walls were white, the furniture was white, the rows and rows of wedding dresses were all white. It was an amazing room. Passionately Ruth said, "Welcome to the bridal chamber." Not being open to the general public, few have access to this room. A few of the Jerusalem House of Prayer staff occasionally come to privately seek the Lord and rest in His presence.

This room was designed for women who are betrothed, to come and freely select a wedding dress. Did I use the word amazing yet? I could feel the sweet purity brimming as I stepped in.

Ruth took a seat in a small white chair, while Darla and I set on a pretty white sofa, with Louann sitting at my feet. Ruth pulled out her Bible and opened to the Song of Solomon. The four of us basked in the reading of the entire Song; the love Song of Jesus and His Bride.

"Who is this coming up from the wilderness, leaning on her beloved?" (Song of Solomon 7:5a)

Me, it was me! I came to lean on my beloved Bridegroom, Jesus. And you are invited as well to come to Him and lean.

We were saturated in Christ's pure, unadulterated love. Just when I thought I couldn't receive any more from the Lord; Louann opened a small bag and brought out a gorgeous white tellite; a precious prayer shawl that she had purchased for me. She unfolded it and laid it tenderly across my shoulders. The weight of the Glory of God was almost more than I could physically take. My three, sweet covenant friends laid their hands on me and prayed the most beautiful prayer I had ever heard.

Sitting in the top floor of the Jerusalem House of Prayer, which sets on the pinnacle of the Mount of Olives, inside the bridal chamber. How much closer could I possibly get to my bridegroom in this phenomenal setting? Jesus is our bridegroom and we are His bride; He longs to embrace us in His Arms and embrace us throughout eternity. I am in love!!! My beloved is mine and I am His, Song of Solomon 2:16a KJV

In the closing of Part Two of this writing, I will share what spending time in Jerusalem has done to me.

It Changed Me -the City of the Great King
Original song by Janet Penney 10/22/2010

Jerusalem my heart does sing,
Over Jerusalem the City of the Great King
When my feet walked down most dusty streets
It changed the very inside of me
Oh Jerusalem city of the great King
When I swam in the Sea of Galilee
I was so free
It changed me-forever changed me

When I bowed low over the place of your birth
When I inhaled where you drew your first breath
It changed me

When I knelt at Gethsemane
Beneath the olive tree
Oh how it changed me

When my eyes beheld the place of the cross- Golgotha
I was lost in- the moment I was lost in the cross

When I placed my feet inside your empty tomb
You were not there- you were not there
My Lord my God you were not there

My risen Savior you were not there
Oh Jerusalem the City of the Great King
Oh Israel over you I sing

There you were born
There you grew up
There you were loved
There you drank your bitter cup
There you were despised
There you died
There you arose
There you will return

On the Mount of Olives You will return
Your feet will touch the Mount of Olives
You will return to Jerusalem
Jerusalem you have forever changed me
I love Jerusalem- I love, I love, I love Jerusalem
Pray for the peace of Jerusalem

Chapter 25

~Airport Chaos~

Our journey out of Jerusalem was as sweet as entering it. Our friend Ruth graciously drove us to the airport in Tel Aviv. All the while she told us stories of her life here in Israel. She spoke of the many avenues that God has taken her on to minister to a certain sect of society. She had never dreamed of all the ways the Messiah desired to channel His love through her. You could feel the pure passion in her heart beating for the people. Without a doubt, Ruth was an abandoned lover of God. Also, Darla was the same, her submitted heart and lifestyle, along with her entire family was a bright shining beacon. It was hard to leave these woman who had so easily found their way into our hearts.

Ruth and Darla, are forever friends who fill a very special place in our hearts that no one else ever will.

They made my first overseas trip so perfectly pleasant. Jehovah Jirah could not have provided two better people to escort us across the land of the Bible. Louann and I will always honor their unfeigned faith and love.

Arriving the mandatory four hours early at the airport, we thought; *what are we going to do with so much time?* To our dismay, we found out very quickly.

I watched Louann struggle to put all our luggage, which included five suitcases, two carry-ons, and two purses on the conveyor belt so we could enter the terminal area. We were bringing home more suitcases than we came with, which only complicated matters. I wanted to reach out and help her but I didn't have enough strength in my hands to do so. Once our belongings were properly placed, she had to remove them and take them to a merging belt and reload them all again. I could see the sweat on her brow along with the exasperation on her face.

As we both were standing there, the airport attendant motion for security. They began to open all our suitcases plundering through them. Louann and I were confused by what was going on. Then they sent for more security and they were speaking Arabic and Hebrew the best I could tell. As they ravaged through all our private things, they pulled out a small hand held blow-dryer, staring at it like it was a weapon of some sort. Louann and I were flabbergasted! The attendant called for her supervisor. They began inspecting the blow-dryer again as they spoke nothing we could understand. About thirty minutes had passed and people behind us were getting frustrated. The supervisor tried to ask Louann where the plug-in-adapter was for the cord. We were more confused than ever now. At that point, they called on the airport phone for someone who spoke English. With half of our personal belongings scattered across the conveyor belt; resembling a free-for-all yard sale, the supervisor told us to find the plug-in-adaptor, *immediately*. Louann dug her hands through our things as if she was digging for gold. The adaptor was only as large as an American quarter so it was not an easy thing to locate. I tried to help as much as I could. After about ten minutes passed, and no plug-in found; Louann asked why it was needed. To the best of their ability to tell us, and to the best of our ability to understand; the allegation was we did not use our blow-dryer for our hair, but for some type of unwarranted weapon. In Israel, the electrical sockets are different than in the United States. You have to have an adapter to plug in things not suited. Since we could not prove that we had used the blow-dryer to actually dry our hair, then it must be a weapon. Now the light came on! Louann, in a semi-panicked tone said, "You can have the blow-dryer, I don't even want it!" Relief came instantly to the situation. What a chaotic mess!

What a disarray of our belongings and our emotions all because of a missing adaptor plug. We had no idea this situation could have happened, or possibly could have been avoided all together. We learned the better prepared a person can be, the easier you go through life's circumstances.

The enemy will always try to knock you off track with the little foxes that spoil your vine. Always trying to snare us with hidden traps.

> "Put on God's whole armor (the armor of a heavy-armed solider which God supplies), that you may be able successfully to stand up against (all) the strategies and the deceits of the devil." (Ephesians 6:11, AMP)

After Louann tidied up our belongings and repacked them, we moved toward the next line to pass our actual *physical bodies* through security. She went through fine and kept walking, expecting me to be right behind her... unfortunately I was stopped by another airport attendant. When he noticed on the monitor the metal plates in both my arms, he became suspicious. With no emotion registering on his face; he briskly pulled me off to a small room and motioned for me to remove the braces. Using my teeth, I did as I was instructed. He then thoroughly inspected every inch of my arms and hands, turning them in every possible way. I tried to convey my injury and the resulting surgery but to no avail. He walked out of the room and returned with another security guard who handled my arms in the same fashion. Having no choice in the matter, here I sat, in a very tiny enclosed room, with two men with two guns, speaking all about me in a foreign language. Can I tell you I was a little uneasy, especially after what just happened with the plug-in adaptor? Close to ten minutes later, they released me. I was trying to put my braces back on and run to find Louann at the same time. She was nowhere in sight! My thought being, because of the dreadful delay, she hurriedly headed to the plane and boarded among hundreds of other people; without even noticing I wasn't there. I just stood there frozen in the middle of this huge, intimidating airport. I quickly came to the startling realization that Louann was carrying the tickets and identification for us both. "Yeshua, where are You?" Just then, in the blink of an eye, I saw Louann abruptly running toward me like a freight train which had run off the track. Whew, I was *never* so glad to see her! I tried to explain what happened as we scurried to another line; the gate of customs. I was beginning to wonder if our four-hours-early-arrival was enough! After showing our passports, we did eventually board the airplane safely, shaken, but safely. We collapsed in our assigned seats and started laughing to keep from crying. Louann said, "It was easier getting *in* Israel than it was getting *out*." I looked straight in her eyes and said, "Let's go home!"

Part 3

After I Left

Chapter 26

~ *Red Cardinal* ~

Shortly after I came home from Israel, I began to feel a stirring in my spirit for change and growth, I sensed a new season was approaching me. My friend Louann, and her husband Roger, had been asked to take a senior pastorate of a church in a small town in Virginia. The Lord had confirmed to them both in no uncertain terms to go. They were leaving in less than ten days after our return from Israel. It was difficult for Louann and I to say goodbye. We had become *joined at the hip*, so-to-speak, after being in Jerusalem together for three weeks, day in and day out.

Roger asked my husband to help them move by driving their vehicle while he drove a U-Haul rental truck. Phillip agreed, and at the last minute they asked me to join. As we approached the outskirts of Virginia, the terrain begin to drastically change. When Phillip say the beauty of the mountains he was in absolute awe. "I could live here! I could sell my house and live here! "Phillip exclaimed. Of course he was expressing such a statement because he had never viewed the mountains before. Remember, we lived in flatland Florida!

After we helped Roger and Louann get settled halfway into their parsonage, we spent a fun day or two with them living, loving and laughing. I had not seen Phillip this happy in years, he was like a little boy with a new toy; his face was glowing. It was a joyous and refreshing time for all us. On the plane ride home, we talked about a return visit in the near future.

Days and weeks went by, and I found myself really missing the closeness that I had with Louann. We talked on the phone daily and always ended our conversation with the subject of Israel. We were forever changed by Jerusalem and by what we walked through together. Once we swam in Sea of Galilee together, there was an indescribable bond. Not even to mention that Louann was *my hands*! She put my food in my mouth then brushed my teeth! You just don't get much closer than that.

Less than a month later, with the holidays upon us; Louann invited me and Phillip to Virginia for Christmas. We joyously accepted the invitation, and purchased our airline tickets right away. We were eager to be with our friends for a week-long visit, and to take in the beauty of the snowcapped Blue Ridge Mountains. Later that week, Phillip was vacuuming our family room, and was thinking about Roger, and all the work that he had to do. He asked God, "Do want me to go Virginia after our Christmas visit and stay a little longer to help him get better situated?" He and Louann had a rented warehouse full of their belongings that needed to me moved, plus the church they were pastoring was in need of a paint job. You have to know this about Phillip; he operates in a strong gift of helps. If he isn't helping someone, he's not happy.

As Phillip is having this conversation with God, the vacuum cleaner cord came undone from the plug, *the one without an adaptor.* As he bent down near the window to plug it back in, he looked outside and noticed a beautiful red cardinal. It was sitting on a bush in our backyard. When he saw the vivid red cardinal it caused him to quiver on the inside, because he knew that it was state bird of Virginia. Looking at the bird he said, "Are you speaking to me God? Do you want me to go by myself and give Roger a hand?" About that time, the lighter colored female bird, came in the yard and landed right beside the male cardinal. So my husband said to God, "Is this sign? Do you want me *and Janet* to go back up there and help them get situated?" He began to weep with this confirmation that God was indeed saying *yes* to his question. God has used animals and nature to speak to His people since the beginning of time.

> "And the dove came in to him in the evening; and, lo, in her mouth was an olive leaf plucked off; so Noah knew that the waters were abated from off the earth." (Genesis 8:11, KJV)

As Phillip was telling me about this meaningful episode, tears filled his eyes. At this point I did not understand the fullness of what he was telling me. I said to Phillip," Why do you feel this is a confirmation for us to go help them?" He began to tell me about Roger's experience that happened less than a month ago. Roger had been sitting outside where he was living, reclining in a lawn chair. He was conversing with God about his recent invitation to take the position of senior pastor at the church in Virginia. As he was asking God if he should move, a red cardinal came and landed nearby. When he saw the bird, instantly Roger sensed that God was speaking to him through His creation. He voiced these words," Father, do you really want me to pastor this church?" About that time the female cardinal came and sat next to the male cardinal, and he knew that he and Louann would pastor the church together. I knew nothing of Roger's experience. But, when Phillip shared it with me, I understood completely; and Phillip's brimming tears then fell down his face and onto his shirt.

As the days went by, we were seeking the Lord about taking a week-long trip to go up to help them. I remember going to church that week and one of my dear friends had on a sweatshirt. Not just any sweatshirt; plastered on front was a male, bright red cardinal with a female cardinal next to it. I stared at this shirt as it was speaking volumes to my heart. I told my friend how I liked her shirt, and the next church service, she brought it in a gift bag and gave it to me. A few days after that, we were sitting with some friends at a small coffee house; we were in a booth facing each other. Early in the conversation, I looked past their heads and onto the wall directly behind them; there was a huge poster of the most beautiful red cardinal. I nudged my husband with my elbow and pointed at the poster not saying a word. He looked at the poster, then our two friends turned their heads and looked at the poster, and when they turned back to look at us they said," Are you guys moving to Virginia?" Totally surprised at their question, I quickly said, "No! But we are going to visit for a few days." And that was the end of the subject. A week later I walked into church again, and a friend of many years, handed me a gift bag. I looked inside; they were six Christmas tree bulbs with each bulb having a bright red cardinal on it! As I gawked at the gift in disbelief, I was speechless. It seemed the birds were following me! I went home that night crying to God and thinking, *what is happening? I feel an unexplainable stirring deep in my spirit about Virginia.*

When God begins to use situations, nature, sweatshirts, posters, even Christmas tree bulbs to speak to you, it's time to sit up and take notice. As these divine moments transpired, slowly I began feeling a separation from the place of my birth; Lakeland, Florida.

I opened my Bible to Ecclesiastes chapter three and read about times and seasons.

"To everything there is a season, and a time to every purpose under the heaven: a time to be born, and a time to die; a time to plant, and a time to pluck up that which is planted." (Ecclesiastes 3:1–2, KJV)

When I read the words, *a time to pluck up that which is planted,* I felt the Holy Spirit's tender grasp around my heart as He whispered this profound truth. I say profound because not only had we lived in the same house for over thirty years, raised all of our children here, we both had solid jobs with the City of Lakeland. Also the majority of our family lives here. Also, we'd been rooted and grounded in our local church for almost a dozen years.

We were not *looking* to be plucked up-we were not *asking* to be plucked up from anything in any way, shape, or form.

A day or so later, I was in the house of prayer in my local church, and I was questioning the Lord about all this. As the prayer session ended, I got in my car, and began to leave the church parking lot. I drive down the street behind the church as I had done literally hundreds of times before.

I said to the Lord, "Am I leaving this ministry? Am I leaving Florida? Do you really want me in Virginia?" I'm gazing out my car window when I looked up at the street sign as I passed. The name of the street was called *Roanoke*. This word jarred me! It jarred me because Roanoke is the city that Phillip and I were flying into in Virginia in just a few weeks for Christmas. I cried all the way home saying, "No, this can't be happening! This can't be happening! No God- this isn't you, this is just my imagination." When I arrived home, I grabbed Phillip and said with a trembling voice, "Did you know the street right behind our church is called Roanoke? "Yes", he replied. "Why didn't you tell me?" I said. "You never asked," was his reply. The next day as I headed back to the prayer room again, on purpose my eyes were searching for the Roanoke street sign. I wanted to make absolutely sure it was real. As I approached the street that I thought was it, I slowed way down as not to miss it. I looked up and read the word *Richmond* on the sign. I did a double take. *Richmond! I thought it was Roanoke?* Slowly I came upon the very next street which was called, you guessed it- *Roanoke*. Now I'm really crying! Richmond is the capital of Virginia. Oh God this is *double confirmation*!

Needless to say, Jehovah Nigad was predicting my future and tugging on my heartstrings. I relinquished my will to go to Virginia, and *not* just for a weeklong visit.

> **"Behold, the former things are come to pass, and new things do I declare: before they spring forth I tell you of them." (Isaiah 42:9, KJV)**

I then called Louann and I told her what was happening; she laughed with great joy. She and Roger thought seriously about what was happening and began to pray. Their prayer was, "God, we don't want them here unless *You* want them here."

We left it at that for a while and kept these things and pondered them in our hearts.

> **"But Mary kept all these things, and pondered then in her heart." (Luke 2:19, KJV)**

The scripture bears out that after the angel of the Lord came to Mary the Mother of Jesus, she kept the words in her heart and wondered what the outcome would look like.

When God places a new vision inside, you will began to see changes in your life. Hold them dear until you see the fruition of it all.

"But when it pleased God, who separated me from my mother's womb, and called me by his grace, to reveal his son in me, that I might preach him among the heathen; immediately I conferred not with flesh and blood: neither went I up to Jerusalem to them which were apostles before me." (Galatians 1:15–17, KJV)

It is not scripturally healthy to share all God has placed in your heart with numerous people. Apostle Paul received the revelation that he was called to preach, but he didn't go around telling other people; he kept those things in his heart and meditated on them. There's a window of time when God may speak dramatically to us, and we to weigh them out; allow the Word of God to divide asunder the soul and spirit.

We went to the Bible and let His Word and His Spirit affirm and reaffirm in our hearts His plan. Knowing this *is* God, and this *is* what He's telling us to do. Then we approached the God-given, spiritual authorities over us. They must distinguish whether or not to say, *yes* to the call and the movement of the Holy Spirit; supporting a true oneness. I've been trained very well over the last thirty-five years of walking with Jesus to operate this way. We tremendously need the benediction from our leaders. If you ask God, He will reaffirm as many times as necessary that you are truly walking in His path. It takes the *all* this to move forward with peace and spiritual satisfaction. We should never move on an inclination, or a fleeting circumstance.

"Trust in the Lord with all thine heart; and lean not unto the own understanding. In all thy ways, acknowledge him, and he shall direct thy paths." (Proverbs 3:5–6, KJV)

Every time I saw a red cardinal, I would acknowledge God speaking to me. The more I acknowledged Him, the more intricate He directed my steps. We miss it so many times, because we don't stop and recognize God moving in the moment. In reality, this is the best way, and the only way, to walk a successful Christian life.

While packing for our Christmas vacation, cardinals were everywhere; in our yard, on our driveway, in our trees, it seemed surreal.

Louann called me about a week before our Christmas visit, and told me that she and Roger were asking the Lord if He moved Phillip and Janet to Virginia, where would they live?"

Shortly after they prayed, a neighbor contacted them and said he had a place for rent right up the street from the church and the parsonage. He wanted to know if they knew anyone looking for a place to live.

As she told me this story, I laughed and told her, "I'll tell you what you do; go down to this house and if there is *red cardinal wallpaper* all in the kitchen I will know it's mine. Ha! Ha Ha!" I sounded carefree and seemed to take it lightly, but I knew it was a very weighty thing.

As she pulled in the driveway of this quaint small home, astonishingly, she saw it was white with red trim and a red porch. She found no red cardinal wallpaper inside, but on the property there was a tall pole with a three-story birdhouse. As she described it to me, I didn't know whether to laugh or cry.

The week of Christmas arrived, and Philip and I landed in the gorgeous mountains of Virginia for our weeklong visit. My husband had never seen snow in his entire life, so we were praying it would snow while we were there. On Christmas morning, we looked out the window just as the snow began to fall. My husband grabbed me with a hug like a five-year-old boy on Christmas morning! Then we both ran outside where we laughed, played, and rejoiced that God had giving Phillip his heart's desire.

Nearing the end of our weeklong visit, Louann asked if we wanted to see the rental home. I was hesitant at first; I felt like God was going to be sitting in the living room.

We did a quick walk through, then Phillip and I went outside to view what looked like about a half-acre of land.

We noticed the stunning slope the home was sitting on. The tall, whispering trees blew in the wind, and snow lightly blanketed the ground. The quiet and stillness of the countryside was different than our backyard in Florida; with so many people, and so many noises.

My husband's arms wrapped around me tightly as I cried, "Do you think God wants us to live in this little house?" Our hearts became completely silent and still. We walked to the front yard and gazed across the street. Just beyond the trees we saw the magnificent, breathtaking Blue Ridge Mountains. It felt rich with the presence of God. Yes! God did indeed meet me there!

I don't know how much time passed until Roger and Louann came outside. They asked if we wanted to walk next door and meet the property owners. We respectfully submitted to the process, the process of God. We all huddled into the warm living room of a charming, picturesque home. Louann introduced us to a delightful elderly couple. As we made small talk, the gentleman pulled out a renter's agreement form and passed it to me to look over. My eyes quickly scanned the paper containing the list of things to be followed. When my eyes got to number seven, I gasped. Number seven read, *No pets allowed.* Now normally that would have not caused a person to gasp, but, less than two weeks ago, we had to put to sleep our family dog of fourteen years. The night of her burial I went to church with red eyes, and was speaking to a friend who said to me, "Why are your eyes so red? Are you okay?" I softly told him that our family dog had died that day. Without any hesitation, he spoke boldly and said, "The dog could not go with you into the new season." He spoke as if he knew every detail of my life, but he knew *absolutely nothing.* His words pierced my delicate, aching heart.

In the cold mountains of Virginia that day, we got up to leave the home of the property owners, Polly and George; Polly tenderly placed a folded piece of paper in my hand. I slid it into the pocket of my long winter coat. When I opened the paper that evening, to my amazement, it was a newsletter from *David Wilkerson's Ministries.* He was giving a teaching on crossing over to new things and learning to die to one's self. As I completed the article, I sat in a daze of delight.

We had taken several pictures of the rental property, and later that night I emailed the pictures to my daughter, Leah who lives in Florida. She walks closely to Jesus and has a fervent prayer life, I trust her completely.

I briefed her on what was happening with the home and asked her to pray for the situation concerning her father and me. Within a few hours she returned my email by saying these words," Mom, I see God all over these pictures! As I was lying in bed nursing the baby, I was praying for you and dad. There was a CD of music playing softly behind me, and the song came on, *Go tell it on the Mountain, that Jesus Christ is born.* As the words came across the atmosphere of the room, my heart jumped, even flip-flopped inside of me as He confirmed, without a doubt, that this home was to be yours. That you and Dad were to leave everything familiar to you and go live on the mountain and declare that Jesus Christ is alive!" She stated that we were *not* to leave the state of Virginia, without solidifying with the owners of this property that we would return and rent this home.

Leah's words were so absolute that it shook every fiber of my being. I thought, *Could this really be happening? God this is so huge, is this real or am I dreaming?*

Life's journey is not so much about finding our place in the world, but finding our place in God. As we die to things we are firmly planted in, allowing God to pluck them up; we puncture through clouds of mediocrity, we fly high towards the dream of God, walking into His abundant life… finding that life is a wonderful journey after all.

Chapter 27

~ *Fire of Delay/Blind Sided by Cancer* ~

———～∿∿oɔɘʏಂⓒʏⓒɔo∿∿——

The excitement that filled the air that day carried me like a floating balloon. I felt light as a feather softly touching the ground. Phillip and I were moving to Virginia to blissfully follow the will of God for our lives. Not only did He speak to us undoubtedly in our hearts to make the move, but God had given us so many signs and wonders to confirm and solidify His plan. We also received a wonderful benediction from the pastor of our local church in Lakeland.

Never move on outward signs alone. Deep within your being God's voice is heard. Some call it a gut-feeling because the knowing comes from the innermost part of us. Webster's dictionary defines gut as, *the most important part of something. The emotional part of a person. A narrow passageway.* The Bible says; *out of our belly shall flow rivers of living water,* John 7:38. So out of our gut or belly the Holy Spirit flows in and out. When a person totally embraces God's rhema word, absolute joy permeates them. Rhema meaning, *utterance.* Actually hearing Him speak on the inside of us, changes everything.

There was so much to do to prepare for this great adventure I didn't know where to start. I was so happy I wanted to tell everybody what God was doing. I felt like Job when he said, *my belly is as wine which has no vent; it is ready to burst like new bottles;* Job 32:19

In this paramount moment, I felt as if nothing could stop me. I was full of vision and completely delighted myself in doing God's will.

> **"I delight to do thy will, O my God: yea thy law is within my heart."** (Psalms 40:8, KJV)

I had never felt so steady and sure of anything in my whole life as I did with this major move to Virginia. Like a rock, His will felt solid inside me. I felt like a rock myself, unmovable.

> **"Is not my word like as a fire? Saith the Lord; and like a hammer that breaketh the rock in pieces?"** (Jeremiah 23:29, KJV)

There are two ways we receive from the Lord; some things are given, and some things have to be bought.

> **"I counsel thee buy of me gold tried in the fire."** (Revelation 3:18*a*, KJV)

Walking in the perfect will of God never comes without a price tag. Things we purchase hold a greater value than things that are given to us. Mainly because we have to invest our money, our blood, sweat, and tears into it. Valuable things, worthy things, like silver or gold have to be refined in a fire to become pure and of good use. People who go for the gold in life by pursuing Jesus, must enter the same type of process.

> **"For thou, O God, hast proved us; thou hast tried us, as silver is tried."** (Psalms 66:10, KJV)

Christ-like character is developed when we, as Christians, are refined in our fiery trials. Like gold, our character becomes more valuable it is when it passed through the hottest fire; so the more effective and useful we become when we do the same.

The refining fire is not *deserved* or *earned*, we simply have to pay the price.

In the crucible of life we find God's nearness. That crucible may include pain, loss of control, intense pressure, and violent change. God's persona is intense.

> "For the Lord your God is a consuming fire, a jealous god." (Deuteronomy 4:24, KJV)

Please allow the preceding foreshadow to bring you into a greater understanding of the following turn of events.

> "He will sit as a refiner and a purifier of silver; He will purify the sons of Levi, and purge them as gold and silver that they may offer to the Lord an offering of righteousness." (Malachi 3:3, NKJV)

Jokingly, I told our grown children that their father and I were about to mount-up on a pair of motorcycles and ride off into the sunset. That was the best way to describe how I felt. I could hardly wait for the great adventure to begin.

Packing, cleaning, and gleaning things from our home, so we could make the most major move of our married life, was exhilarating and exhausting. In the midst of all the motions and emotions, things were moving along quite well. That is until one evening while washing the supper dishes, I felt a wave of weakness sweep over me. I had not been feeling well for the last two weeks. I thought maybe I had some type of flu-virus or something. I began to sway back and forth at the kitchen sink until all my strength left me. I dropped to the floor like a wet dishrag. A few minutes later, Phillip found me in a crumpled pile of weakness. Gently, he lifted me up and carried me to bed. My chest was hurting and I realized my heart was beating erratically like it had done in the past. Phillip loaded me into the car and took me promptly to the emergency room of Lakeland Regional Medical Center. When I told the triage nurse that my I had pain in my chest, and that I had a history of premature ventricular contractions, she whirled the wheel chair into the emergency ward where they quickly began further examination. After inconclusive tests on my heart, I was admitted for observation.

In my room the next day, the doctor said that all tests proved that my heart was fine. "However," he begin to speak of my complete diagnosis, "In going over your chest x-ray, I noticed a spot on your left lung," he said. "Because it seemed such a small and insignificant finding, I really don't think it necessary to biopsy it at this point." the doctor continued. "We can keep an eye on it and wait about three months and see if there is any change in the dime-sized tumor. Or we could biopsy it now while you are here in the hospital," he said.

I expressed that I would rather wait, but it was a good thing Phillip was there. He spoke up and said, "No, I think it best we have the biopsy right away."

I started feeling nervous as the doctor spoke of the procedure. He assured me that it would be very simple. He would insert a heavy gauge needle in my back, push it through the cartilage of my rib cage, puncture the lung, and then withdraw a small amount of the tumor. He informed me that there was a minute chance my lung could collapse during the process. Honestly, I felt a little anxious hearing his words, so he had the nurse give me a pill to help me relax.

Lying face down on the table, wide awake and *not relaxed at all*, I felt the insertion being made in my back and the thrust that it took for the instrument to reach its destination. I gasped from the searing pain. I began to grow faint and nauseous as I struggled to say," I can't breathe!" Quickly they began to view the cameras to see if my lung had indeed collapsed. It had not. They began administering medicine while trying to turn me over on my back and place me in an elevated position. Halfway up, I began to vomit, which made things worse. I felt like I had just been stabbed! I guess because I had been. And I thought this was a "simple procedure." I wondered, simple for whom?

Checking out of the hospital the next day, I could barely move. The soreness of my back and chest was near an unbearable level. Although the results wouldn't be ready for seven days; I was confident they would reveal no serious complications. At the most, pneumonia that could be treated with antibiotics. I wasn't sure what was going on with me. The only thing I was sure of was that I belonged to God and my life is in His hands.

Upon arriving home, I noticed cars parked in front of my house and people all over my yard.

I had forgotten that my family was helping us with a moving sale. We planned it after God confirmed our move seventeen amazing times.

We were selling our furniture, dishes, etc., plus my car and even our home.

We were moving to Virginia the following week. Well actually, I was flying up alone a week early, and my husband would drive our vehicle up in about three weeks. He had to stay behind to tie up all the loose ends on this side of the journey.

I was so excited to get into our new home located high up in the mountains. I had recently bought some wall paper and border that I was going to apply, while I was alone waiting for Phillip to arrive.

On the seventh day since the biopsy was taken, I was feeling well enough to drive myself to my doctor's appointment for the reading of the biopsy results. Before my 4:00 appointment, having some money from the moving sale, I decided to do a little shopping for my new house in Virginia. Happy as a lark, I went from store to store picking up a few red knick-knacks. Red, black and white was to be my new color scheme since God had used these impressive little red cardinals to speak to me. My last stop was our local department store before I headed for the doctor's office. While shopping, I saw my sister- in-law, Tammy, who worked at the store, and she was just getting off work. As we talked and walked toward the exit, she invited herself to join me at the doctor. I told her that would not be necessary, but she insisted.

We were called back to the exam room and were seated. The doctor walked in and peered over his glasses saying, "Mrs. Penney, do you smoke?" "No" was my response, "I never have." As he hummed and grazed over my paperwork, he shockingly said that I had a malignant tumor in the lower lobe of my left lung. It was about the size of a Canadian dime. He stated that he had to operate immediately. The cancer was very aggressive and he must schedule surgery as soon as possible. Out of my mouth I said without even thinking, "I'm moving to Virginia on Thursday, I can't!" In case he didn't hear me, I said it again. I looked across the room into Tammy's eyes; she was just as stunned as I was. The thoughts in my mind turned to all of the words God had spoken to me concerning the future. I mean we were on our way out of an old season of life and leaving everything to fulfill the plan of God, *next week!*

"What if I don't want to have surgery?" I said. "Then you have less than two years to live," the doctor stated bluntly.

The doctor had me follow him up to the desk where I was to obtain my records. He said, in no uncertain terms, that as soon as I arrived in Virginia, I was to check myself into the hospital and submit to the surgery right away.

"Do not wait more than two weeks, Mrs. Penney, two weeks. This cancer is spreading fast," he said.

I sat in my car in front of his office after Tammy had driven away. In the stillness of the moment, my mind tried to grasp what had just happened. I felt numb, completely numb. It was as if all of time stood still. I fumbled for my car keys, cranked up and begin to drive robotically. I woke up half way to the place where my husband was working. As I turned the car off in the parking lot, I just sat there. Slowly I reached for my phone and called Phillip. "Please come outside, I need to talk to you," I blankly said. When the words were spoken out loud that I had lung cancer and had less than two years to live without surgery, there was a stone silence that filled the atmosphere of our vehicle. I don't know how many minutes passed until Phillip voiced, "What are we going to do? Your plane flies out in six days."

Mindlessly, he reached for his phone and dialed our pastor's number. The advice we received in that moment was the only thing that made any sense in this whole day.

"Janet, you don't want to go into the new season with this in front of you. You want to stay in the old season, deal with it, and then leave it behind you."

That was exactly right. This was wisdom speaking for sure. We should not move to start a new life, with the first task being to admit myself into the hospital for cancer surgery. Reality was setting in, this was factual, and I had to make some quick, major decisions. My head was still spinning when I went to bed that night and tried to regroup on all the plans that I needed to change.

At 2:30 a.m., I was abruptly awakened by intense pain in my chest. It felt as if someone had doused my lung in kerosene and then struck a match. I began screaming horrifically. I weakly limped to my dresser and picked up the papers from the doctor's office that I had been given earlier that day. My eyes scanned for his telephone number. As I dialed it, I crumpled over on the desk and cried uncontrollably. The answering service responded to my serious cry and the doctor was on the line within a matter of minutes. "Your lung must have collapsed. Meet me at the emergency room right away," he said.

The nurses heavily sedated me upon entry due to the intensity of pain. I awoke the next morning in a private room, finding I had been admitted into the hospital. Eventually the doctor came in and said that my lung had not collapsed as it seemed. They immediately began more tests to see if the cancer was anywhere else in my body.

After the third day of testing, I lay in my room meditating on one of my favorite scriptures in the Bible; Psalms 24. The room was dark and it was almost time for the sun to rise. How I needed the Son to rise in me. After all these upsetting tests, I really needed the Son of God to lift me up. I was thinking, *I refuse to lose!* Within my mind, I started quoting the verses (Psalm 24:1-10).

"The earth is the Lord's and the fullness thereof; the world and they that dwell therein. For He hath founded it upon the seas and established upon the floods. Who shall ascend unto the hill of the Lord? Who shall stand in His holy place? He that hath

> clean hands and a pure heart; who hath not lifted up his soul to vanity, nor sworn deceitfully. He shall receive the blessing of the Lord, and righteousness from the God of his salvation. This is the generation of them that seek Him that seek thy face, O Jacob. Selah. Lift up your heads O ye gates and be ye lifted up, ye everlasting doors; and the King of Glory shall come in."

When I got to the final line, I stopped and said out loud, "Will you come in King of Glory? Will you come in and help me please?"

In that precise moment, the door of my room swung open and there stood a man in a long white doctor's coat. The light from the hallway was shining bright behind him. I could not see his face well because it was dark in my room. He said, "There is no bone cancer, no brain cancer, there is no trace of cancer other than in your lung; we are going to proceed with surgery."

"Wow God!" I said out loud. "That was quick!" I laid my head back into my pillow and continued to meditate on the rest of the verse.

> "Who is this King of Glory? The Lord strong and mighty, the Lord mighty in battle. Lift up your heads oh ye gates, even lift them up ye everlasting doors and the King of Glory shall come in."

I stopped right there and said, "Keep on coming in King of Glory," and all of a sudden my door swung open again. This time it was the nurse who informed me that there was a mysterious, unexpected opening in the surgeon's schedule for 1:30 p.m. that day. She told me not to eat or drink so I would be ready for the operation. Then she was briskly gone, in the same manner as the doctor. My heart was racing with the anticipation. My foremost thought was; *the quicker they remove this tumor, the quicker I can recover and move to Virginia and enter my new season and my new life.* I finished meditating on the remainder of the verse,

> "Who is this King of Glory? The Lord of Hosts, He is the King of Glory. Selah." (KJV)

I lay there quietly basking in the delicate, morning light that now began to seep through the curtain. Tears were falling softly onto my pillow as I thanked God for quickly coming to my rescue. The Lord of Hosts was swiftly moving, more swiftly that the cancer in my body.

The King of Glory showed up just for me; Jehovah Shammah the Lord Is There, Ezekiel 48:35.

He will do the same for you in your moment of crisis if you simply invite Him.

Maybe you are not fully grasping what had just transpired. You see, the doctors had previously informed me that the cancer would spread rapidly and time was of the essence. He also informed me that there were many patients ahead of me who also needed surgery; and that it could be several weeks before he could schedule me. In the same moment, he apologized, but it was the best he could offer. Obviously, by what had just happened in my room, it was truly the Lord of Host-Jehovah Sabaoth, Mighty in battle, fighting for me. What a faithful God we serve! The King of Glory kindly told me that my faith in believing and inviting Him into this situation pleased Him very much.

"And he said to her, Daughter, your trust and confidence in Me, springing up from faith in God has restored you to health. Go into peace and be continually healed and freed from your distressing bodily disease." (Mark 5:34, AMP)

God uses interventions in our lives in various forms, whether it be through medicines, or surgeries, vitamins, etc. Don't debate with God in the ways He chooses to help you. Walk in the process trusting Him all the way.

As Phillip and I stood at the operating room doors, where we had stood only months ago for my double wrist surgery, I grasped his hand; with my arms still in braces. Softly I spoke of my apprehension of having the surgery. I knew that as I came out of sedation, the pain would be exasperating on my body.

Phillip's tender, compassionate brown eyes were looking deep into mine as he told me everything would be okay. Then I was suddenly whisked away behind those cold, and too familiar, operating room doors.

This rare lung cancer was not fed by tobacco smoke, yet it was extremely aggressive. For the sake of saving my life, the surgeon deemed it necessary to remove the entire lobe where the cancer was. What I thought was going to be the removal of the tumor was actually much more. I sadly understood that I would require an insurmountable time for recovery. The right lung has three small lobes and the left lung has one small lobe on top and one large lobe below; the lower one was removed. I was told within a year or two my body would reach its optimum health.

Here I am a psalmist, always singing and praising God with my breath, and now that very breath I need to glorify Him was being abated.

Maybe this was just all a bad dream. This could not actually be happening to me. My world was spinning so fast I didn't have time to process my situation. I tried to determine how life would be with part of my lung missing. Would I ever be the same again? Would I be able to run and play with my grandchildren? Could I sing prophetically over the nations again? Would it be possible to sit at the keyboard and pray hours in a house of prayer? Or would I be reduced to only praying aloud for minutes?

Upon awakening hours later, I found myself in Surgical Intensive Care. There was a massive air purifier behind my bed so I could breathe the purest air possible. I awoke in indescribable pain in my chest and extremely shallow breathing. Groggily I opened my eyes and saw three men standing at the foot of my bed. I thought, because of sedation I was having blurred vision. I actually rubbed my eyes and looked again. What I thought was my husband, was being seen in a set of three. I opened my eyes the third time and tried to focus intently. It was three men! My husband, his brother, and our son. They were all standing in the same position with their arms crossed. They each had brown hair, brown eyes, a mustache, and all favored each other. When they saw I was awake, they surrounded my bed. Fighting for breath, I whispered to the nurse, "How big is the hole in my side? It had to be big enough to reach a hand in and cut off my lung with scissors." At this everybody laughed but me. I closed my eyes and was sinking into a deep sleep. I didn't want to wake up again because the horrendous pain and gasping for breath. I felt like I was in a plastic bag and all the air was seeping out.

I had a breathing tube, a drainage tube, oxygen, IV's, and a morphine pump all attached to my body. I didn't know if I could do this, or even if I *wanted* to do this. Part of my body had been taken from me. "How could this have happened God? On Friday, I felt fine, and now, just three days later, part of a major organ was cut off. What a horrible weekend! "Why, God why?" I cried as I drifted into a state of perfect peace and rest.

Within the confines of my deep sleep, I saw the most brilliant white dazzling light. It was warm and inviting. Somehow I knew this was the entrance to eternity, to immortality. I wanted to run as fast as I could to that light. I thought, *if this is death, then I want to go!*

"Have the gates of death been opened unto thee? Or hast thou seen the doors of the shadow of death?" (Job 38:17, KJV)

Seeing this light meant only one thing to me; eternal life. I asked for sleep medication to because of the intensity of the pain and the shallowness of my breathing, for it seemed beyond tolerable for me. How could I have had this life-threatening happenstance? I wanted to die. I had been through so much pain and suffering in the last few months; my body felt weak as well as my heart and soul.

Unfortunately, they couldn't give me anything to sleep because it would slow down my breathing; I had to be awake in intensive care as much as possible so they could monitor my progress.

The only thing that sustained me through these gruesome days was the joy of the Lord deep in the soul. My heart was constantly on Jehovah Rapha, the Lord my Healer.

"For I am the Lord that healeth thee." (Exodus 15:26b, KJV)

I knew there was destiny and purpose inside of me. Knowing that no matter the obstacles, that came my way, I could overcome through Jesus Christ. I could never compromise the integrity of who I am, or the integrity of God.

Our bodies are created to have all our organs intact, when we lose them, there is an immense suffering. There is also a grieving that our emotions must process; which I was to dramatically discover later.

Out of Surgical Intensive Care and now in my private room, I told Phillip put on my door, *No visitors.* I was so wired up with tubes and IVs and machines and heavily medicated, it was all I could do to literally get through each moment much less each hour and day. Surely I didn't want anyone looking at me in this struggle. Yet there was one young lady named Kelly, who was adamant on seeing me, and totally ignored the sign on the door and determinedly walked in.

Kelly and I began to talk of this sorrowful delay in my life, knowing that I could not move to Virginia as planned. She spoke of a book entitled, *Fire of Delayed Answers,* by Bob Sorge. The book speaks of how sometimes we have the plan we think is God, then discover He has a greater plan. We end up being delayed on our human time-table. Yet all the while our Heavenly Father brings purposeful delays that refine us. In the end, patience has been developed and our character has matured.

As Kelly was sharing this with me, I could hardly focus due to the morphine drip, but my heart latched onto her every word. Within minutes, she jumped from her chair, and said "I'm going to go buy the book right now!" Then she was gone as abruptly as she came.

During my recovery time at home, I opened the book and begin to read. The author told of the refiner's fire sent from God. He spoke of buying gold in the fire found in Revelation.

"I counsel thee to buy of me gold tried in the fire, that thou may us be rich; and white raiment, that thou may be clothed, and that the shame of thy nakedness do not appear; and anoint thine eyes with eye salve, that thou mayest see." (Revelation 3:18, KJV)

Also the author told of Job's perseverance and spoke of his pain being worth the gain. He brought so many insights into my soul, and my heart began to develop at an alarming rate. There was a true fire burning out my will, my desires, and in its place; a sweet aura of purity, hope and patience.

> "Spectacular achievement is always preceded
> by spectacular preparation."
> ––Author/Pastor Robert H. Schuller

My husband postponed my airline ticket for six weeks until I was able to follow the flight of the red cardinal. My body was trapped in this season of delay; yet this preparation time was conducive to what God wanted to do through me in Virginia. Resolving my thought life on this intention, was indeed challenging. Looking around my home stacked with boxes of our belongings, and the barren picture-less walls, I wanted to scream and run away. Yet that was impossible. With pen and ink I found my release in this song; as I lay, weak and broken before my God and His toasty Refiner's Fire.

Fire of Delay
Original song by Janet Penney 03/11/2011

Every step I take
Every move I make
His eyes watching me -my Creator
I have learned the brevity of life- it's but a vapor
The fragility of life were so fragile
There's no promise of tomorrow
In the fire, the hot fire of delay, He holds me
I cannot have my way
So I wait in the fire of delay
He's holding me there, keeping me there, maturing me there
In the fire of delay
I am buying gold in the fire of my personal pain
Through my suffering I am learning His ways
I cannot escape the hot fire of delay
He is molding me, shaping me in my pain

As I cry out Jesus, as I cry out his name
It's so precious to me
He's doing things I cannot see
Inside me
My will -my way they die in the flames
So many things cannot be explained
You got a plan God so much bigger than mine
And I trust you
As I wait, in the fire of delay.

Sometimes we learn more in losing a battle, *or so we think we lost,* than in winning.

Practice letting patience have her perfect work.

Patience-(adj) able to remain calm and not become annoyed when waiting for a long time, or dealing with a difficult problem.

"Consider it a sheer gift, friends, when tests and challenges come at you from all sides. You know that under pressure, your faith-life is forced into the open and shows its true colors. So don't try to get out of anything prematurely. Let it do its work so you can become mature, and well-developed, not deficient in any way." (James 1:2–4, MSG)

The battle that we think we lost can place us in a whole new arena if we let it. Never try to get ahead of God, there is great value in the waiting. We desire to walk in His will and attain the His promises, yet we must have the fruit of patience operating in us to receive them.

"For ye have need of patience, that, after ye have done the will of God, ye might receive the promise." (Hebrews 10:36, KJV)

"But they that wait upon the Lord shall renew their strength; they shall mount up with wings as eagles; they shall run, and not be weary; they shall walk and not faint." (Isaiah 40:31, KJV)

Chapter 28

~ *Quiet Mountain* ~

Living, loving, and laughing was the motto on every plaque inside my new adorable home; nestled on the side of the mountain in Critz, Virginia. I had wall paper in the kitchen with these words, in black, red, and white. Our house was popping with color of the new season, which had finally arrived.

People told me that it was so dolled up that it looked like a picture in a magazine. I was happy, and progressively healing with the daily intake of the clean mountain air, enjoying a somewhat carefree life. Faithfully, I gave myself to prayer in the newly established prayer room at our joyous God-assigned church.

Earlier, when Phillip and I flew up in December to celebrate Christmas in Virginia, I had taken a walk on the street in Critz. I was telling God that it might be hard for me to not live near water since I immediately noticed the absence of a body of water in the mountain landscape. I didn't realize what a culture shock was in store for me. For the thirty years we lived in Florida, a peninsula surrounded by the ocean, my home was very near to a beautiful lake. Walking around this body of water often was my quiet time with the Lord. It brought me solace from my busy days as I savored each moment. As a psalmist, *He leads me beside still waters and restores my soul*, and for me, this was literal.

I was in quandary about this while walking that story-book winding road that cold December morning. Then, I heard a faint noise off in the distance. I continued my down-hill pace as the sound became louder; all the while expressing to God my water dilemma. Louder and louder the strange sound grew, until I came upon a large ravine to my right. As I glanced through the snow-covered trees, I saw it... *water flowing down from the* mountain *and splashing on huge phenomenal boulders.* Once I laid my eyes on the water, I about jumped out of my skin! Without question, I had to go down there. I trudged through the brush covered with delicate, fresh-fallen snow; and cautiously placed my feet on one of the gorgeous water-worn rocks. Fresh water flowed from my eyes, just as it did the mountainside. I opened my mouth bubbling these words, "Thank you Jesus, thank you Jesus, You love *me* so much to give me the very desires of my heart, and I love *you* back!

Eagerly, I anticipated meeting with God on the unyielding, solid rock. Connecting with nature not only allures us closer to Elohim-our Creator, it also brings healing to our tattered emotions.

Everybody needs beauty as well as bread, places to play in and pray in, where nature heals and gives strength to body and soul. –– John Muir

Visiting my water brought, *peace, peace, wonderful peace, flowing down from the Father above.* It was while sitting there one day that God reminded me of what I had spoken in Jerusalem. I said "I'm going to write a book and call it, *Journey through Jerusalem-With no Hands*". In that very moment, on that God designed rock, He began designing the book in my heart.

> "And the Lord answered me, and said, write the vision, and make it plain upon the tables, that he may run that reads it." (Habakkuk 3:2, NKJV)

God writes the gospel not in the Bible alone, but on trees and flowers and clouds and stars. ––Author unknown (but commonly attributed to Martin Luther)

All was quiet in my home, in my heart, and in my soul. God was refreshing and healing my lungs with the pure mountain air, my wrists were better and I was able to so much more with my hands. I was in love with the freshness of life, in love with the new people He placed around me, and in love with Him. I was forever grateful for His intervention in saving my life. I felt I had been given a second chance to live. If the doctor had not found the cancer *accidently* through a chest x-ray, I would have moved here and within a short period, could have been found dead all alone on the mountain. Nurses tell me often that lung cancer is *never* found this early; and cancer cannot be seen on an x-ray. It had to be divine that it was diagnosed like that and dealt with. I totally agree it was, truly I am a *grace-case*.

After a few months of solitude on this amazing quiet mountain, I sensed a shift inside of me which gave me a foreboding feeling. I spoke nothing of this to anyone but tried to joyfully continue on my journey.

My children and grandchildren came to visit me, and I would take them down to the mountain stream to play in the water. Other family and friends visited us from Florida as well. My parents came from Texas for a refreshing get-a-way. We even had some dear friends from Indiana come to partake in the landscape of God. They all enjoyed the breathtaking views of the mountains, and the stream where I felt most encompassed by the presence of the Creator.

Spring was leaving, summer had come, and fall was just ahead, and I was happy. Yet in the innermost part of me there was sadness. When the time changed on our clocks, and daylight was shorter and nights were longer, my days of brightness felt shorter, and nights of darkness begin to feel longer. What was happening God? Why was I feeling such alterations of emotions? How could I not be happy in this amazing new season with everything changing and everything becoming new? Now, on my quiet mountain, detached from noises, sounds and people; peace seemed elusive to me. As nightfall loomed its shadow over the quiet mountain, there was an ominous presence invading my life.

Chapter 29

~ *72 Dark Hours* ~

———⟶◦◦◦◦◦◦◦◦◦◦———

Seventy- two hours is three days equal. On a three day fast, Queen Esther changed a nation. In three days Jonah's heart and mind was transformed inside the belly of the fish. In three short days our Lord and Savior Jesus Christ conquered death, hell, and the grave. I recall my three day journey of having being diagnosed with cancer on Friday, then waking up Monday with part of my lung surgically removed. It's amazing what can transpire in such a short amount of time.

The seventy-two hour story you are about to read is going to be the most transparent chapter of my life. I must allow myself to become vulnerable, realizing that healings occur in transparency. Not just my healing, but yours as well. Transparency gives people the opportunity to see what's really going on inside, and find where God is located in that process.

It was early August 2011 when I found myself feeling desolate; recognizing the one-year anniversary date of my wrist accident was upon me. I was missing my family, my home, and the life my husband and I worked so hard to build in Florida. I was dwelling on the fact that all of it was gone. Besides beginning to feel lonely, I found myself vulnerable to discouraging thoughts. No one knew all the suppressed emotions pinned up inside me; up until this point; neither did I. It was like my soul had landed in a stupor of dejection. My eating habits began to change. Normally, being adamant of my dietary stance since becoming a certified nutritionist years ago, I was now allowing anything on my plate. This was so far from my usual lifestyle of self-discipline. I felt sluggish and rapidly began to gain weight in a short period of time. "What's going on God? I thought I was born for such a time as this, and I was brought into the Kingdom for such a time as this? But what is *this*?" I said.

Wanting to be true to myself, and keep intact my identity in Christ, yet I felt insecure.

I felt foreign that my thought-life was spinning out of my control. It seemed my disposition was changing. I was soon to discover the full meaning of the word *holistic*.

Holistic means all-inclusive, concerned with wholes rather than the dissection of parts. Our person is not only a body, but we are a spirit being as well and we possess a soul which is made up of our mind, will and emotions. One cannot ignore their mind, which is housed in the soul, and think they can detach it from the rest of who they are. Yet, if they do, they will never become well and whole. The Bible is the only available power to divide our soul from our spirit. Without the Scriptures we cannot have clear distinction between the issues of the heart, and issues of the mind/soul.

"For the word of God that speaks is alive and full of power (making it active, operative, energizing and effective); it is sharper than any two-edged sword penetrating to the dividing line of the breath of life (soul) and (the immortal) spirit, and the joints and marrow (of the deepest parts of nature), exposing and sifting and analyzing and judging the very thoughts and purposes of the heart." (Hebrews 4:12, AMP)

Due to all the traumatic events of the last few months, my soul had become impaired. Through my ignorance, and busyness, I had compromised my own *total*, or *holistic*, well-being. Because I was still involved in my Bible reading, prayer life, and was actively engaging in true worship, I thought I was okay. I couldn't figure out why all these emotions were surfacing at the same time. I tried many times to suppress them, yet another would come in its place. In this interlude of some sort of depression, I just let the thoughts and emotions freely come. As I did, the tears flowed freely with them.

I began dwelling on our dog Chrissy, a part of the family for fourteen years, whom we had to bury shortly before we left Florida. Weeping swept over me as my heart ached for her companionship; I longed to run my fingers along her beautiful long, blonde coat. I moved to Virginia just after her burial and I never gave myself time to grieve.

I found myself lamenting for our son Mitchell, who recently underwent a heartbreaking divorce after ten years of marriage. When the divorce transpired eight months ago it broke me in a million pieces; I felt like I got a divorce too. At times I would cry so much for Mitchell's separated family I could barely function. Our two precious grandchildren being so young and innocent were of my utmost concern. The brokenness became a great agony in my soul. Unfortunately, I didn't allow myself to process the deep scarring pain of emotion. I never took the time then because it hurt so bad, but now, on my quiet mountain, I had to take the time.

My attention would turn to my aching wrists cause from the traumatic accident which had thrust me into shock and disturbed my equilibrium, the violent shake had severely handicapped my emotions. The cold weather here in Virginia made my wrists hurt, only causing me to think more on the accident. The metal plates in them caused so much discomfort. My limitations, such as still not being able to open a bottle of water after almost a year, were almost maddening to me. I thought surely I would be better by now. I found myself in such a sad state of mind, and I began to take notice that I was crying over these things daily.

> **"For his anger endures but a moment; in his favor**
> **is life: weeping may endure for a night, but joy**
> **cometh in the morning." (Psalms 30:5, KJV)**

This scripture was true, I would not cry incessantly. I knew this was not a forever state of mind for me. Yet that night; the encroaching darkness seemed to become profuse. Only small glimpses of joy would harness my heart and give me steadiness to go each day.

The nostalgic moments of the precious ministry of the house of prayer which I had so diligently given myself to in Florida were becoming vague. The two full years of training, teaching and helping to build the *Tabernacle of David* in the hearts of people, now was only a memory. Now, I am experiencing the emotional detachment from the team of mighty intercessors, my treasured friends. I worked so closely with these people in the house of prayer in Lakeland; now they were out of my reach.

Yearning for my children and grandbabies at my core, increased daily since this major geographical move. Each time I went to a store and came near the children's section, I found myself quickly turning away. It hurt to think of how our physical closeness was gone. It wasn't until I had no children laughing in my new home, not one toy in the house to pick up, that I felt the penetration of loneliness and seclusion from life I once had.

Then there was the destructive, whirlwind, weekend with lung cancer; including the abrupt removal of my lung less than six months ago. This traumatized me more than I realized. The confines of shallow breathing would send me into panic attacks, and I had to use sublingual meds and/or oxygen or a nebulizer. I was no longer singing as hard and long as I did before the cancer. Singing had become one the biggest parts of me, now it looked like the smallest part and my heart was broken.

My life had incorporated such drastic changes. How horrifying all these things were feeling now. While I was walking each one of these circumstances out, they didn't seem unbearable. Since they were consecutive traumas, there was no real time to process them individually, which contributed greatly to this latter distress. I was oblivious to my distressed emotions. They didn't feel so life-shattering then, but now, the accumulation of a years' worth of undealt with and unprocessed emotions were invading my ever-present mind.

"When I remember these things, I pour out my soul in me: for I had gone with the multitude, I went with them to the house of God, with the voice of joy and praise, with the multitude that holyday. Why art thou cast down, my soul? And why art thou disquieted in me? Hope thou in God: for I shall yet praise him for the help of his countenance." (Psalms 42:4–5, KJV)

There were so many traumatizing events that happened *all* within *one short year*. It seemed these major things could have happened over a decade, but not one single year!

This was not the way it was supposed to be! This is not the way I should feel! Can you relate? Has your life taken you down paths that you thought would be a high-flying adventure? Then it turned out to be a nightmare pushing you down into a pit of despair?

The climb *up*, generally begins with asking why we are *down*. Don't be afraid to ask God, why you're in your situation today. Seek the Lord for your ultimate help. What you do in the thick of the trial is really going to matter a few months down the road. In our abrasive times, we have to know He is smoothing us out. In our dry-dying moments; He is Living Water. When rain is plentiful; water is an **after**-thought, but during a drought; it is our **only** thought.

> "As a white tailed deer drinks from the creek; I want to drink God, deep draughts of God, I'm thirsty for God- alive. I wonder, 'Will I make it; arrive and drink in his presence?'" (Psalms 42:1–2, MSG)

Let me interject right here that these hard, dry, moments did *not* come to *stay*, they came to *pass*. If you are in such a place now in your own life, please know, that help is on the way. Jesus is the Great Deliverer.

I had never experienced such emotions to this degree. I had moved from a very busy city life, to a secluded spot, away from everything and everyone familiar. Had God strategically placed me here? Such immediate changes were not only exciting, they were becoming painful. The Holy Spirit made me keenly aware that adjustments were essential; I had to deal with the fragments of my soul.

To grow is to change and to change is to grow.

Getting back to that August day; I sensed things began to feel abnormal to me. This extreme gloom is now an unwelcomed visitor that does not want to leave. Even with the television on I can't connect with what is showing. I am not a television person and I have very little interest in it; yet, I had it on to drown out the voice of sadness within me.

Sometimes in life we have more questions than answers, which should cause us to run into God and wrestle it out.

For sure things are wrong, very wrong, and I needed answers! Yet I did not feel the strength to wrestle anything or anybody. Upon awakening to the fact that this is depression; I knew that His ankles were my only anchor. Bowing low enough to clinch the feet of Jesus and pray was my only way up.

"I don't think that anyone goes down as low as those who go high." --Beth Moore

When we are cast down, we tend to ask questions that we would not normally ask. Providentially, this takes us into a deeper dialogue with God. As I was at home just a few days into this depression; I was in a brief conversation with God that was reaching the deep in the caverns of my soul. I was very melancholy when a knock came at my front door. It was my dear friend and beloved pastor, Louann. As she made her way into my small quaint home in the mountains of Virginia, she found me as I lay despondent on the sofa. With her weighty and unexpected words she said, "Pack your bags, we are going to the hospital." "No way!" I said, as I rolled over and put my back to her. "This is bigger than both of us and you need professional help. I am going to check you into the psychiatric unit at the hospital." Louann said.

That morning I had told my husband to please remove the gun from the house before he left for work. Then he called Louann to tell her of these daunting words that I had spoken. She was aware that my soul was downcast. So when Phillip told her of my words, she prayed and made contact with her spiritual authority for counsel. She said "I don't know what to do with Janet, thirty years in ministry and I don't feel I can help her."

The godly advice was given to quickly get me to a place of help and safety, where people are trained and qualified to deal with such substantial issue. She identified that I was *not* the Janet she knew and cared for, so she began to make huge strides to bring me back to myself.

> **"Every purpose is established by counsel; and with good advice make war." (Proverbs 20:18, KJV)**

> **"Where no counsel is, the people fall: but in the multitude of counselors, there is safety." (Proverbs 11:14, KJV)**

Endangering, foreboding thoughts can easily seep through a depressed mind. I barely recall telling Phillip those words, yet they were foremost in his mind. I don't think I was actually suicidal, but I had enough wits about me to know I was emotionally sinking fast, and having a gun in the house, even if it was there only for our safety, was not an object I remotely wanted within my reach.

I am a person well acquainted with life, joy, happiness and truth. I know Truth and the power of Him, for Jesus is The Truth, The Life and The Way. Yet what I was experiencing seemed like anything but life, joy, happiness or truth. "God, what truth are you trying to unveil through all this emotional pain and confusion?" So began the fight for the sacred space of my soul.

When you have been presented with truth, that truth demands a response.

With Louann's deep concern for my well-being and I mean *deep*, I reluctantly got up and forced myself to throw some personal belongings in a bag. I cried and babbled the entire forty-five minute drive to Martinsville Memorial Hospital. "I changed my mind; I don't want to go through with this!" I shrieked. It was to no avail. She was adamant about checking me in to the psychiatric ward. She assured me the people there were great in their area of expertise. Formerly Pastor Louann had worked in this very hospital and knew many of the staff. So she was confident I would be in good hands. Humph! She was- but I was not! I squawked and squealed, rocked and reeled my way through the admittance part of the journey. Behind the private curtain, as they surveyed me, and asked about one hundred questions, I shivered with fear of the unknown. After the allotted time of surveillance, I was diagnosed with Clinical Depression and Post Traumatic Stress Disorder.

Unfortunately too many people don't understand what these conditions truly are. The Christian world tends to believe that if you are depressed, in any form, that you are demon-possessed or have yielded yourself over to sin. Please allow me to clarify. Depression for me was caused by the sudden traumatic events which battered my mind and emotions. Beyond my control, my stress hormones and chemicals of my brain became unbalanced. The miss-informed person may think my symptoms gave the implication that an evil spirit came to me and whispered in my ear and tempted me to become sorrowful and dejected. No, that would be satanic oppression which can develop into demonic depression. When a follower of Christ opens their eye- gate or ear-gate to the voices of the devil, then gives themselves over the those voices, that would be sin, which would invite the satanic oppression in. Then the more the person yielded to this realm, surely they have welcomed extreme darkness inside their soul, which eventually would blend into their spirit and at this point could actually become demonically depressed or even possessed. I am sure many of you have heard horror stories of people who have experienced an exorcism and coughed up evil spirits and their voices become distorted. But a true believer should be able to acknowledge the difference. In my case, I recognized my condition was not brought on by any open gate to wickedness. I pursue righteousness and godliness more than I can express. Jesus has been and always will be the center of my life. I chase after purity and holiness with every fiber of my being. Yet, if I had allowed myself to remain with this disorder without seeking a way out, I believe, that over time, I could have succumbed to complete and total demonic depression. Simply because my thoughts would have drowned me in my own sorrow, and to the death of me, the real me, I would cease to exist.

"Put on the whole armor of God that ye may be able to stand against the wiles of the devil." (Ephesians 6:11, KJV)

Though a righteous man falls, he gets back up! This is not just referring to falling into sin. If you or I fall into *anything* that would detour us from wholly walking after God, we immediately need to recognize the hindrance, so we can get up and back into our rightful place.

Think of it this way; every time you patch a leak, a rainstorm comes and reveals the weakness. Rain will continue to pour in trying to weaken the entire structure. The important thing is to strengthen the weakness before it springs a leak that cannot be repaired.

Shortly the room would be ready for my seventy-two hour stay. I literally clung to my friend and wept. "Don't leave me in this dreadful place" I pleaded. "I don't belong here! I am a spirit-filled believer, a teacher of the gospel, prophetic psalmist, a godly woman; I am a grandmother for heaven's sake and a good one!" Well, if you know Louann, she buckled down, gritted her teeth, and somehow with the greatest compassion I had ever seen in a human being, gave me the assertion I needed to go the duration. Her eyes brimming with tears and so much love, gave me the comfort I needed. How I thank God for my friend-my covenant friend.

Honestly, I thought that Louann would think less of me. I mean; she was standing next to me when my wrists were broken and watched the providence of God. I was one of the head intercessors in our church and the director of our house of prayer, the one person who was called upon to be an ambassador to Israel. I was the one she walked the streets of Jerusalem with and closely observed as the Spirit of God come upon me as I sang prophetically all over the land of Bible. She saw my determination to not be defeated but to be resilient. I had sensations of degradation, not coming from her at all, but it was placed in my mind by the enemy. I realized how factual this scripture in Revelation is.

> they overcame him by the blood of the Lamb and by
> the word of their testimony, and they did not love their
> lives unto the death." (Revelation 12:10–11, NJKV)

The devil was coercing me to accuse my own self as he backed up his plan. But, I knew I could overcome and would overcome by the blood of the Jesus that was spiritually covering me.

Inside my room were two other women. One was cornered up in her bed with the covers up to her neck with an empty look in her eyes; she was muttering something that didn't make sense. I quickly turned away. My other roommate sat quietly on her bed watching my every move as I placed the few things I was allowed to possess into a tiny drawer. Slowly I positioned my comb, my toothbrush, my Bible, and a small notebook along with a family portrait that I scavenged from by purse before they took it away. By the time I turned to sit on the bedside, the lady observing me was blatantly sitting on my bed. I was jolted at the site of her and swallowed hard. It made me uncomfortable to have this sick stranger so close to me. Her words were, "God sent you here. I was praying this morning for Him to send someone to help me. I need a friend that will understand." I figured out that when she saw my Bible she assumed I was a believer. Her assumption was correct. But I did *not* want to help her. I did *not* want to be her friend; I did *not* want to be in this place at all! I am the one supposed to be here to **get** help anyway, not to **give** it! What we consider crisis in our lives can sometimes thrust us through the doors of potentiality. It forces us to make a move. You are going to move, either forward or backward, but *you are going to move!* We all need contact with other people to survive. We cannot be an island unto ourselves. God did not create us that way. The Great High Priest, Jesus is touched with the feelings of our infirmities and has designed us to have such a deep dependence on Him. We may not know how deep and how wide that dependence can go until we end up in places that seem so obscure.

> "Neither is there any creature that is not manifest in his sight:
> but all things are naked and opened unto the eyes of him with
> whom we had to do. Seeing then that we have a great high priest

that is passed into the heavens, Jesus the son of God, let us hold fast our profession. *We have not an high priest which cannot be touched with the feeling of our infirmities;* but was in all points tempted like we are, yet without sin. Let us come boldly unto the throne of grace, that we may obtain mercy and find grace to help in time of need." (Hebrew 4:13–16, KJV) *emphasis mine*

It is comforting to know that Jesus sees all and knows all that goes on in our lives, nothing escapes His attention. He is moved by our troubles and understands what it's like to have infirmities of any kind. To me, my situation and circumstances were alarming; I never thought I would see the inside of a place like this. For those who know me personally you may be shrinking with trepidation, sadness or even disappointment. It's okay. I learned years ago during a horrendous hit from the enemy, this prevailing truth, *the greater the trial-the greater the victory.*

Despite my resolution to keep to myself and submit to this frightening and humiliating process, I found my heart touched with my new friend's need. Deborah* was also a Spirit-filled believer struggling with depression. Life can bring some really great surprises in some really unfortunate events. She asked me what church I attended. As I handed her the church weekly bulletin that was still inside my Bible, she combed through it she said, "Pastors Roger and Louann Moore! I know them!" Wow, now the surprises were becoming very interesting. The call to line up and receive medications was being announced. What in the world!? What have I gotten myself into? This looked like a jail agenda to me. I was beginning to feel like I was in prison. I got in line and the people there scared me. No one talked to the other, but just had blank expressions. Some muttering what sounded like insanity to me. I guess it was. I was ready to pack up my few, *very few*, belongings and go home. After taking my meds, which was mandatory that I take in front of them, I enquired of the nurse what I was swallowing. "Anti-depressants and a sleeping pill" she said. I had never taken an anti-depressant in my life. Going back to my forlorn room, I went to the bathroom to brush my teeth and prepare for bed. As I was standing in front of the sink when

I looked up and saw that the mirror in front of me was a flat piece of shining metal and not a mirror at all… *yikes*, I am in jail!

Wake up call was at 7:00 a.m., then another line up for breakfast. Being so drugged up from the pills they gave me the night before I could hardly hold my eyes open to eat. Seated at a table with one of my roommates, the one with the empty eyes, and an unshaven man who talked excessively to himself, well, let me just say this, I felt sick, sick, sick. The guard who attended us as we ate, informed us of the time and that group therapy was to start. *Therapy! Group therapy!* I did not want to be in the same room with these people let alone spill my innermost guts with them in a therapy session. None the less as the group of about a dozen men and women gathered I found myself among them, yet in an attitude of solitude. My body was present but I wondered about my heart and soul. I didn't know where they were.

In actual fact, Clinical Depression is a chemical imbalance, a shift in chemistry within the body. It is a treatable condition. With the proper medication and counsel one can be victorious over it. Psychologically, depression is anger turned inward. When traumatic events take place in our lives, for instance, the death of a child, a divorce, or rape, these occurrences injure our emotions. Things we did not expect or ask for make us angry deep within because our lives are altered in an undesirable manner. Yet the element of anger may get buried deep in our soul- which is our mind, will, and emotions. Because the current circumstances may have happened suddenly, we use our energies on fixing the existing problems that we can see, like preparing for the funeral of the child who died. While under the surface, our blemished emotions are subdued. Often times they're not recognized until months or even years later. There they remain concealed under our busy lives or our embarrassment to express our hurt and anger. Mainly because we are angry with God is the reason we do not admit it. We have to ask the infamous questions "why God? Why did *You* let this happen?" For me, the things I questioned were, "why did my wrists get broken while I was worshipping You? Now I have permanent damage, including the loss of grip in both hands? Why did I get lung cancer when I am a singer for You? Don't you know God that I need my hands to play the piano? Don't You know I need all the breath I can get to sing out loud like I love to do?" I was never aggressively angry at any point with my circumstances, but because I am human, the emotions originated. If the truth be told, it's okay to be angry with God, He can handle it. If you are in relationship with someone, is there not a time in which something happens and you get angry? Use the anger as a release valve, and then be done with it.

> **"Be ye angry and sin not: let not the sun go down upon your wrath."** (Ephesians 4:26, kjv)

We are in relationship with our Heavenly Father and I am sure He gets angry with us periodically. We are made in His image, so should we expect anything less? Without the understanding of this, we are ashamed of our unholy thoughts and feelings that we tuck them away somewhere lodged in our soul forever, or so we think. Even if we desired to express them, we don't know how.

If at first you do not seek professional help, find a trusted friend or pastor that you can talk to. Someone you can confide in. And if, in your counsel with them, you discover that you are actually depressed, run for the *cover of God!* To our demise, the church at large, places such a stigma on depression. They think you are weak in your faith, when in reality it has little to do with your faith.

If prayer, fasting, worship, and Bible reading would prevent depression, I would have not experienced it.

Generally speaking, we need more insight into this matter. The body of Christ very proficiently can minister to the spirit of man, while the other areas go lacking. Let's stop treating someone with depression as if they have the plague. Someone told me at the onset of my encounter that I should not let people know about this trial. That it would be the death of my godly reputation. Good! Now Jesus can be more alive in me because He

is a man of no reputation. People are looking for the genuine. The many facades that people guise themselves under need to be dismantled.

Everyone, including young children can recognize hypocrisy; which brings disillusionment and disappointment. We allow ourselves to become tainted with duplicities in our own heart. All the while, as mere humans, we simply crave the depths of authenticity.

Give me one valid original person any day, rather than a room full of pretentious people. It is when we bare the truth of our soul and become raw and completely open that miracles take place. Dare we take off our rose- colored glasses as we view people? Even people we esteem as prominent. We are all just flesh and blood. We should learn to live purely, from the inside out. Never misrepresenting our own selves, and not buried under mixed motives or hidden agendas.

> "But He made himself of no reputation and took upon Him the form of a servant and was made in the likeness of man." (Philippians 2:7, KJV)

Truth reigns in the highest place, we must allow it. How many kings do you know who stepped down from their throne? How many fathers do you know that gave up their sons? Since my Lord Jesus set the supreme example of humility, I venture to think that I cannot fail in imitating Him.

I have discovered an entire new level of maturity and understanding since walking this walk. One of my counselors in the hospital told me this was not a great place to be but I would be grateful that I came through here. The degree of compassion I now embrace is beneficial and very rewarding in my life. There are certain destinations we can never arrive at unless we walk certain paths. I can genuinely say this is one of those paths. If you have never been affected by depression or been around someone who is, there really is no way for you to fully understand what it is like. I remember telling my daughters when they were pregnant with their first child that they could not comprehend the measure of love that you feel for your baby until you hold them in your arms. And thus it is true with depression. You cannot begin to grasp the depths of despair, anguish and grief you deal with unless you have been affected by it. Rest assured that our Mediator, Jesus Christ, knows.

"He is despised and rejected of men; a man of sorrows and acquainted with grief: And we hid as it were our faces from him. He was despised, and we esteemed him not. Surely, he hath borne our griefs, and carried our sorrows; yet we did esteem him stricken, smitten of God, and afflicted." (Isaiah 53:3–4, KJV)

Nothing could have prepared me for this intense battle for the sanity of my soul. I came face to face with this monstrous thing and when I had that brief suicidal thought I recognized how serious it was. If you, or someone you know is depressed, please seek professional help. Pastor Louann obtained godly advice when she was fully made aware of my situation and that's why she was knocking on my door that day. Whether she realized it or not, she saved my life.

Please pay close attention to the words of someone you think may be depressed. Words like; "I wish I wasn't alive" or "nothing is worth living for", or the words I used, "remove the gun from the house." These are not normal statements. It is a cry for help. Suicide is always, always a cry for help!

Because this topic brings an overtone that is shame-based, most people tend to hide and just put their head in the sand like an ostrich. The thought of being judged because people don't understand, only adds to the problem. But by the giving **of** yourself, you get the help you need **for** yourself.

By keeping open communication with God, I knew while sitting in the psychiatric ward that I would soon get better, and that God was going to use me to help eliminate the stigma that is attached with depression. I also had a knowing that He would use my story to help others walk into their own freedom from emotional distresses.

As I bare the nakedness of my soul, I implore you to take in these words of advice. God can and will clothe you with His grace and peace. He wants to be a *covering* for you in your struggle. Some of the articles He may clothe you with, adjoined with prayer, will be medication and professional counseling. There are many highly trained and anointed people out there prepared to help you. If you break your leg and while it was healing the doctor recommended *physical-therapy* to help you walk, would you go? Sure! We would use whatever means available to promote health right? Or if you had cancer, they would offer you *chemo-therapy* to help. Well my psyche or mind, which is housed in my soul needed, psychotherapy. My therapist was also an ordained minister from the Baptist denomination and was an associate pastor in nearby North Carolina. He had a call on his life to educate himself in this field. My heart is eternally grateful that he answered the call. This was the most amazing six months of my life. I was made so free. I learned to operate in what I knew, instead of what I feared.

With God as our fortress and high tower we can conquer anything that comes our way. This includes depression, and PTSD, which I will talk about in another section. Let Him instruct you and guide you into the steps you are to take and be prepared to take those steps, wherever they lead you, even if it is to a counselor or even a psychiatric ward.

The hospital staff encouraged me to give myself to the counseling sessions and not withhold anything. God has placed so much power in the human mind. Let's utilize it for our gain, not our pain.

Don't miss your therapy. Don't miss taking your medications. Stay in the Word of God, listen to worship music and pray. Don't allow loneliness to creep in. Try to surround yourself with good company. Stay connected to God. The more I did these things, the stronger I became, and was confident that God was paramount in this process. I strongly believe in the interventions of God.

At the end of my six months, my therapist stated that of all his clientele, I was among the few who had made the most significant improvement. He said that if he had not seen with his own eyes my raw, disheveled condition he would not believe I was the same person. Please note that I had to press willingly through embarrassing moments to make significant strides forward. If I did it, so can you. You see there is a hope and a future for me and you as well.

**Finding yourself depressed is not a disgrace. The disgrace
would be if you did nothing to help yourself come out.**

On the second day of my hospital stay, the story of David in Ziklag
came alive to me. In I Samuel 30, it tells how distressed David was
after finding Ziklag in a ruined heap. He cried out so much that verse
four says he had no more power to weep. Have you ever felt this way?
The pain and sorrow is so heavy that you cry and wail until you have
no strength left or any more tears. Yet by verse six the scripture tells us
that David encouraged himself in the Lord, his God. As I was reading
this story lying in my bed I thought to myself, "That's me alright. I am
like David, but too bad I can't encourage myself like he did. I am way
too depressed." My surroundings were also making me feel worse. Just
then the nurse wheeled in an oxygen tank to administer my breathing
treatment. Remember, less than six months ago, I had part of my lung
removed due to lung cancer. As she was placing the plastic breathing
mask over my face, she said that I had visitors. "Oh no! I don't want to
see anyone nor do I want anyone to see me!" I was soon to discover that
swallowing my pride would not give me indigestion, but it would give me
freedom and clothe me with humility.

As I sat with my pastors, Roger and Louann, in an assigned visitor's
room, Pastor Roger proceeded to share what the Lord had given him
for me. It was 1 Samuel 30:6, where it tells the story of David and how
he had to encourage himself. Yes, this is the exact scripture that I was
trying to chew on for the last few hours. Hmm imagine that. Then he
went a little further in the chapter where David asked the questions;
shall I overtake my enemy? Shall I even try? In verse 8 God said to him;

Well that's all I needed to hear that day. Those words brought me the courage to move forward in this process. Having enough strength in my spirit and mind to pursue and conquer was critical. The illumination that came from the light of God's word helped to brighten my life enough to believe that the enemy of my soul was defeated, and that I would without a doubt, *recover all!*

After my seventy-two dark hours there in the psychiatric unit and after being around men and women who were just like me, I learned some valuable insight. Even though some of them were seemingly worse off than me, I could see their trapped emotions behind empty eyes of anger and pain that had never been dealt with. Such was the case with my new friend Deborah, who had been molested by her brother and his friends when she was a small child. She had embedded within her the painful emotions of shame and anger and thought there was no need to talk it out with anyone. But oh the need was very great within her. I encouraged her to talk with God as things surface, even though He knows it all already. He loves it when we initiate a real conversation; He wants us to cry out of the depths of our being, holding nothing back.

I continued to pursue and press in toward all the help I could possibly obtain. Do not let the suppressed emotions of hidden anger fester inside your soul; they can be detrimental. Seek the help you need from the trusted people God places in your life. Don't look for God too high up or too far away, He is near; Immanuel, God with us. Depression is not the end my friend. Essentially it can be a new beginning like it has been for me. In actual fact, those last three days, those seventy-two dark hours, have catapulted me into a greater dimension of life, into a search for absolute truth and wholeness, not just for me, but for others too. The compassion of Christ is at an all-time high inside me and as I continue to be a house of prayer, to worship and intercede for people, I know that a greater compassion for the emotional disturbed will flow out and compel me to help them. Isn't it amazing that our trials and tribulations have the ability to introduce us to the gifts and callings of our lives?

In suffering many things, I have learned many life languages. Our lives exhibit periods of purpose that are undeniable, that change us forever. This is one of those vast periods of time for me. I am learning to trade my warfare for His wealth. Nature always fights for survival not destruction. Let the hurt and the Healer collide, then rise up and fight for what belongs to you. Attach yourself to your eternal purpose and live.

> "Trust in the Lord with all thine heart; and lean not unto thine own understanding. In all my ways acknowledge him, and he shall direct thy paths." (Proverbs 3:5–6 KJV)

It is not only the Word of God that I carry, but the Word of God that carries me.

Chapter 30

~ *Challenges* ~

Post-Traumatic Stress Disorder (PTSD) is defined as, *a severe anxiety disorder that can develop after exposure to any psychological trauma.* It is caused by having witnessed a severe injury or death or experienced an event that brought you injury or the threat of death. PTSD changes the body's response to stress. It affects the chemicals and stress hormones that carry information between the nervous system and the brain. Some common symptoms include recurring memories, nightmares of the event, anger, irritability, insomnia, and depression. Professional therapy and the proper medication have been proven effective. I am a living, breathing example. So if you feel you are being brave by ignoring what might be PTSD, please allow me to bring enlightenment.

> "My people are destroyed for lack of knowledge." (Hosea 4:6, KJV)

My desire here is to help bring awareness. The enemy of our soul wants to harm the internal dialogue that we have with our Creator. If we continue to walk in confusion and fear in our mind and emotions, we will struggle all through life. When we are at war within our own self, we are at war with those around us as well. Facing up to any psychological disorder is proving to yourself and others that you are truly brave. I am certainly not an expert on these subjects by far, but I have experienced enough that I can display empathy. Our afflictions should not take us completely down, instead it should take us down to our knees in prayer. If we embrace the pain and lay out our case before God, instead of trying to escape it, we are guaranteed in the following Bible verse that He will turn our grief and sorrow into joy and dancing.

"I called out to you Oh God, and laid my case before you: 'Can you sell me for a profit when I am dead, auction me off at a cemetery yard sale?' When I'm 'dust to dust' my songs and stories of you won't sell. So listen! And be kind! Help me out of this!' You did it: You changed my wild lament into whirling dance; you ripped off my black mourning band and decked me with wildflowers. I'm about to burst with song; I can't keep quiet about you. God, my God, I can't thank you enough" (Psalm 30:8–12, MSG).

Learning to face what wounds us, opens the door for the Healer, Jehovah Rapha, to heal us. Don't allow lethal strongholds to remain in your life. Tell Jesus, the Lover of your soul, everything; get real with Him and real with yourself. Stay linked to God. In our modern age of communication through telephones and texting, we lose intimacy with people; don't lose your intimacy with Jehovah Elohim, your Eternal Creator, the One worthy of your love and attention. Every detail of your life concerns Him. Jesus is an everyday God. He wants to share your life, no matter how crazy it is.

Unfortunately, people tend to categorize any psychological issue as *insanity*. Not so! It's just that people encountered *insane situations* and actually survive; and the brain has to process what happened. I overheard someone say; *everyone deserves the right to go nuts sometime.* This might carry some truth to it, as long as you strive to get out of the nut jar.

This is not a sin problem where there must be repentance; on the contrary, the traumatic encounters creates neurological pathways in the brain that must be shut down so the electrical impulses are re-routed to a part of the brain that will not cause panic or activate the "fight, flight, freeze" part of the limbic system.

> "And a highway shall be there, and a way, and it
> shall be called The way of holiness; the unclean
> shall not pass over it." (Isaiah 35:8*a*, KJV)

This scripture bears out that God makes a *high*-way that no evil destruction can travel on whether it is physical, psychological or demonic.

> "He opens and no man shuts; and shuts and no
> man opens." (Revelation 3:7*b*, NKJV)

It is vital that we ask God, the creator of our entire anatomy, to shut off things that are causing harm in our brain and to close the pathways of trauma and anxiety and begin to declare and establish life and health. Allow Him to use the interventions given to mankind to channel this highway of holiness and wholeness.

After being diagnosed with PTSD, and prior to my admittance into the hospital, I was aware of negative psychological issues existing in me but I wasn't sure of what was happening and PTSD was the furthest thought from my mind. I just knew something was off balance in my thoughts. I first realized it in Jerusalem while attending a service during the convocation. Louann and I were seated on the front row with thousands of people in the service. Right after the worship portion of the service had ended, I heard a clambering noise next to me. A lady was taking her seat, and as she did, the chair slid out from underneath her, and people quickly gathered to help break her fall. As soon as I heard and saw what the clatter was about, I ran as fast as I could to the ladies' room and began to shiver and cry. In my mind I was right back in the very moment of my own incident. At that time, it had been less than a month since my accident which occurred also during a worship service and had broken my limbs. Now, with this new frightening episode affecting me in this way, I knew my emotions had been harmed. Throughout my walk with God, I have always desired to continuously upgrade the quality of my life. Yet this problem seemed to be degrading the quality instead.

Rational Emotive Behavior Therapy was the name of the therapy my psychotherapist used in my case. REBT focuses on resolving emotional and behavioral disturbances and therefore enabling people to lead more productive lives. It was developed by an American psychologist and psychotherapist named Albert Ellis in the mid 1950's. In his study he discovered that it is not so much the disturbances we acquire, but how we perceive and internalize them. There is an element of the Therapy that is called the ABC model.

"A": You have an experience or happening.
"B": You have a belief about what happened.
"C": You react to that belief.
It basically reveals that B causes C, instead of A causing C.

Like as in my case:
<u>"A"-the experience-</u> Someone fell on me and knocked me backward and my wrists were broken. A surgeon repaired them, and over time the pain minimized, and with few limitations, I now can use them. Sounds simple and easy right? Sure it does, in just the physical state. But I am more than a physical body. I am a spirit and I possess a soul. So, within the confines of my soul or my psyche lies the problem. I had never had an experience such as that before. It was a new road for me to walk and it has changed my life in so many areas. Now, being on the upside of this journey, my desire is to help others that maybe walking this same road and they do not have a clue of what is going on inside them.

Let's take a gaze into my soul for a minute. Here I am in my church, a safe haven for me at the altar of God; surrounded by people I have fellowshipped with for many years, people I love and respect. My heart is engaged in sweet, pure worship toward Jesus. The very next second I am on the floor, trying to figure out what happened and how I got there. I did not see the person fall, because my eyes were closed the whole time. I was thrust suddenly into a state of panic and shock.

Shock (n)-A disturbance of the equilibrium, a sudden violent mental or emotional disturbance, to surprise with terror or horror, a state of profound depression of the vital processes caused by severe crushing injuries or burns, a state of being disturbed, a violent shake or jar; a concussion.

Because I was experiencing shock, time had no relevance; neither did the people or the place I was in. All I knew was that I was tremendously disturbed in my emotions.

"B"- the belief about the experience- What happened to the precious communion I was engaged in? Where was I? Where was God? What was going on? All this was flooding my soul with great velocity; I could not comprehend this and I was confused. This should not have happened to me! *Ever!* Not only was my body damaged, my soul realm was damaged as well. Our mind, will, and emotions are much more complex than our physical bodies.

"C"- the reaction to that belief- All these disturbed thoughts and feelings were now trapped inside of my psyche and there they would lie, until, in the not too distant future, they would begin to find a way of escape. This escape could be good or bad according to how I decide to structure my believe system. The hurt you feel when you have to face the truth, is not as bad as the hurt you will feel if you don't face up to the truth. Sub-consciously, I was afraid to go back in the church, afraid that something would happen. Of course, I did eventually return, but even then, I would not go up front to the altar. I always found myself standing back. At first I didn't realize it; I thought I was fine. Until I looked around one Sunday morning during the altar portion of the service and I was just about the only person still in my seat. Then the light came on and I had a vague idea something was wrong.

No matter how we obtain the negative issues, it is the irrational beliefs and behavior patterns we accrue which causes the dysfunction and the disorders in our lives. As long as we allow these to live in our soul from the past, in the present, or the future, they will continue to harm us.

> **"Men are disturbed not by the things, but by**
> **the views which we take of them."**
> **--Epictetus-Greek philosopher**

Any undesirable event can wreak havoc on our minds. It is how we learn to cope with them that will bring the healing. REBT is generally used for anxiety disorders, of which I had due to a culmination of distressing personal events.

We have an enormous need to interact with other people that we may survive in this world. No one can be an island unto themselves and live healthy. We are all human and should not avoid relationships. We are made in the resemblance of our Heavenly Father for a reason. We need God and God needs us and we need people.

> "So God created man in his image, in the image of God created he him; male and female created he them." (Genesis 1:27, KJV)

> "And the Lord God said, it is not good that man should be alone; I will make a helpmeet for him." (Genesis 2:18, KJV)

These scriptures bear out that it is not good for man to be alone. This is not simply relating to a husband/wife relationship as most think. But truly it is not good that any person be alone in his walk of life. When a person seeks incessant solitude it is more than likely because they are depressed and not physiologically healthy. Each of us must learn to open our own release valve and beneficially express ourselves to trusted mankind.

As I submitted myself to the recommended counseling, I gained relief and minimized drastically my emotional distress. I learned to be very candid with my therapist. I learned as well that linking up with the resources that God wonderfully placed in my life was an absolute. Also, being encouraged to create a solid support system of family and friends around me really made the difference.

Maybe, like me, you have experienced an event or many events that you had no control over. Specific places make you uncomfortable. I have to admit to you, after I was injured at the altar during church, I was disturbed in my mind. My heart wanted to go and be in God's presence and be among His people, yet that was not were the problem was. You can imagine my emotional struggle. Well think about this. As a devout Christian for over 30 years- how could I *not* go back to church, how could I *not* kneel again at the altar? The church is designed to be a place of comfort and peace, not of fear and pain. Our hearts are designed to have a deep dependence on the Great Shepherd of the church, so if in any way you feel violated with harm, there is a definite problem and it should be expressed to someone trustworthy. Let us always be moving forward into true and healthy relationships, not backward into the distressed areas.

We all have room for growth and improvement. God is forever calling us upward and onward to the next level that He has for us. It is through challenges that we grow and find out that we have more to us than we realized. Whatever does not kill us makes us stronger, if we allow it. If the enemy sends his Goliath into our personal battle, it magnifies the value of our trial and the value of our victory. Amen?

I recall when I first started directing the House of Prayer two years before the accident, I was on the keyboard playing and singing for hours at a time. Over a period of a few weeks, I strained my voice. Yet I was so committed to fulfill the role that God had placed me in that I kept on singing. Eventually I caused fibrous tears on my vocal cords. The pain caused me to remain completely silent, it was agonizing. Silence can be uncomfortable, but I was comforted when the Holy Spirit brought to my attention that He was still using my words from the prayers I had already prayed. Words and sounds never die, they continually reverberate throughout the atmosphere I know, but I still wanted to be a voice in my world around me.

**"Words have set whole nations in motion… give
me the right words and the right accent and I
will move the world." --Joseph Conrad**

My silence went on for five solid months. Can you imagine no talking, no singing for five months? And here I was the director of the house of prayer and could not even pray out loud. Yet it did not stop me from standing my watch. I was still there every single time. I began to channel all my energies into playing the keyboard. Again, I played for hours at a time. After a while, my wrists developed small knots which I discovered later were cysts. I was in so much pain as I played. I was encouraged to see a massage therapist to help remove the knots, which initially brought on even more pain. But over the course of about six weeks my wrists did began to heal. If it wasn't one challenge, it was two. Ever been there? I learned that in suffering many things, you learn many life languages. The situation forced me to use music CD's. I could not sing or play, yet I was determined to give my all at what I knew I was called to do. Life presents challenges all along the way, but we keep going. Keep doing what we know to do.

> "Do what you can, with what you have, where you are." ––Theodore Roosevelt

> "No test or temptation that comes your way is beyond the course of what others had to face. All you need to remember is that God will never let you down; He will never let you be pushed past your limit; He will always be there to help you come through it." (1 Corinthians 10:13, MSG)

> God won't give you more than you can take. You might bend, but you won't break.

In our human existence, we will never accomplish more than our thoughts will allow us to. This is why the enemy works hard and long to disrupt our mental faculties; so he can interrupt our holy conversations with God. He wants to have our minds absorbed in ourselves and our problems so much that we cannot even think straight. Each day we need to create space and set the atmosphere in our home, our heart, and our soul so we can remain in constant communion with Jesus. In turn this will bring our thoughts and the intents of our heart into alignment with His written word. The word of God is a light; it can illuminate our way so we can see where to go and what to do. Sometimes, to find the brightest light, we must pass through the deepest darkness.

> "Be careful for nothing; but in everything by prayer and supplication with thanksgiving let your requests be known unto God. And the peace of God, which passes

all understanding, shall keep your hearts and minds
through Christ Jesus." (Philippians 4:6–7, KJV)

If you invite Him to come, He will come and bring you peace. God will remain faithful to you. The Holy Spirit desires to help you personally in every circumstance that you allow Him to. I adjure you to call out to God today. There is no requirement on the length of your prayer. You don't have to be long-winded with God, sometimes only a small breeze will do, just a simple prayer from the heart.

On the one-year anniversary of when my wrists were broken, I was on the front row of church, with my eyes closed worshipping God, when I realized it was the precise time of the event. I began to feel sick in my stomach. I literally ran out of the sanctuary straight in the restroom and knelt at the commode. My mind was back in the moment. It was real my friend, very real. All I could do was whisper, "Jesus", and He was there. He instantly began to restore my soul. This is comparable to being a diabetic, in the fact that you cannot help the chemicals your body produces. As I said earlier, trauma affects the chemicals within us, our stress hormones. So in any case, whisper his Name.

"The Lord is my shepherd to feed guide and shield me. I shall not lack. He makes me lie down in green fresh tender pastures. He leads me beside the still and restful waters. He refreshes and restores my life, myself; He leads me in paths or righteousness, uprightness and right standing with Him. Not for my earning it, but for His name' sake. Yes though walk through the deep sunless valley, of the shadow of death, I will fear or dread no evil, for You are with me. Your rod to protect and Your staff to guide, they comfort me. You prepare a table before me in the presence of my enemies. You anoint my head with oil, my brimming cup runs over. Surely only goodness, mercy or unfailing love shall follow me all the days of my life and through the length of my days, the house of the Lord and His presence shall be my dwelling place." (Psalms 23, AMP)

As long as we walk on this earth, Jehovah ROHI is constantly restoring our lives. His goodness and mercy are truly following us. It is not a one-time event. Just recently, I had to take my husband to the emergency room a for a heart problem he was dealing with. While we were in a small examination room waiting for his admission to the hospital, I was standing in the doorway and I overheard a nurse at the nurses' station in her conversation. She was on the phone with someone talking about the young lady who was next to us. She was describing her depressed condition along with her meds and symptoms. Everything she was saying sounded just like what was going on with me at the time of my admission to the psychiatric ward. I watched as they wheeled this sad, despondent young lady on a gurney, all the while speaking of the evaluation she must encounter with the psychiatric department. My heart grieved with the all too recent pain and memory of myself. I quickly left my husband's side and walked as fast as I could to my car, slammed the door and limply laid my head on the steering wheel and began to cry. This had thrown me right back in the moment. I felt sick and wanted to vomit. Oh how I wish I could vomit all that had happened to me right out of my system! I wish it could be that easy. But it is not. My emotions had been scarred by what I thought of as a shameful and painful process of merely my own admittance into the hospital psychiatric ward.

After getting my husband settled in a room in the cardiac unit at about midnight, I left him to go home. As I walked inside my dark house all alone, my insides were still shaking with what had just happened to me. Gloominess was closing in on me and tears flowed as I dressed for bed. When I pillowed my head, the only thing I could say was, "Jesus hold me, please hold me."

I realized these were classic symptoms of PTSD. I knew I had to address them. Avoidance is allowing your mind to think one thing, so you won't have to think of something else. We humans are very good at this.

The very next morning I voiced what had happened to my therapist and a close family member who knew my story. After releasing the fear and pain of this strong difficult memory with them, my whole demeanor changed. I realized what could have become a secret struggle and taken me down into a deeper emotional valley had to be released out of my mouth and out of my soul. Secrets kept inside are lies in disguise but you only deceive. After a few days, I found myself somewhat relieved of the situation. Not to say it will not happen again because the healing of the soul is a process; but if I continuously strive to overcome every single challenge, I will. And so will you in Jesus' Name. One of our truest obligations is to bring a greater balance to our lives.

Sometimes there are times when just a faint whisper to God is all we have the strength for and that's okay. It really is okay. In these moments you have like this, ask Him to hold you close and He will. Remember we are forged in the crucible of life. God can only do *through* you, what He does *in* you. Your future can bring great opportunities to help someone else who is being challenged. Most trials do not come to stay, they come to pass.

Our great God and King will wrap His loving arms around you and embrace you. This alone will give you the strength and comfort you need for survival in any challenge large or small, that you may face.

With any area of your life's problems that tend to make you anxious, remember, it's only a growth opportunity. Instead of hiding your head in the sand or trying to run away from these challenges, embrace them; be eager to gain all the blessings that are hidden in the dark, difficult times. Beautiful photos are developed in a dark room, we are no different. Don't waste your precious energy regretting the way things are, or thinking about what might have been. Just live in the moment and search for The Great High Priest and His heart in the middle of any challenging circumstance that may encumber you. Your difficulty can bring you to your destiny.

"Seeing then that we have a great high priest that is passed into the heavens, Jesus the son of God, let us hold fast our profession. We have not a high priest which cannot be touched with the feeling of our infirmities; but was in all points tempted like as we are yet without sin. Let us therefore come boldly unto the throne of grace that we may obtain mercy and find grace to help in time of need." (Hebrews 4:14-16, KJV)

The great Creator of the universe is creating and designing your life by an original design. All the personal things that you go through are making you who you are. The literal scars on my body from the surgeries are only a testimony; my pastor said in like this, "They are trophies of His grace". We are fearfully and wonderfully made. So don't try to copy your life after someone else that may have succeeded in the same area that you are dealing with. Allow the Holy Spirit to carve you into an original masterpiece. Oh, the enemy of your soul will fight you for this status, but at the end of the day, when you win, it will all be worth it.

Have you ever heard of the expression, *blind faith?* Well, that blind faith has eyes of its own that can pierce through the darkness of your trials and lift you up. There is so much power in the human soul that was placed there by God, tap into it. What you are doing right now is truly going to matter in your future. In your furnace of affliction, you can go down in despair and become *pitiful* or you can rise up and become *powerful*, but you cannot be both. During the hottest trials of life, Jehovah God will bless you.

> "Blessed is the man that endures temptation: for when he is tried, he shall receive the crown of life, which the Lord hath promised to them that love him." (James 1:12, KJV)

Even at writing the completion of this section, I am facing a brand new challenge. For several months, I have been having debilitating migraine headaches and dizziness, so my doctor is scheduling a head CT scan, to eliminate any suspicion of cancer. She informed me that lung cancer is prone to spread to the brain. With these severe symptoms, I have to write a while, then lay in a dark room with an ice pack on my head, yet even at that, the relief is minimal. I then return to my desk to write more. Just today I have had to retreat about four times to my bedroom. Only a few weeks prior I had to take a PFT, Pulmonary Functioning Test, to gain clearance for a minor surgery. The test revealed that, due to scar tissue that has developed on my lung from the cancer surgery, it has advanced to COPD, Chronic Obstructive Pulmonary Disease, including chronic bronchitis and emphysema. My Pulmonary specialist said I would have to remain on the new prescribed medicine for the rest of my life or continue to struggle daily with my breathing. The only thing with this new medicine, one of the side effects include voice changes. As I sing the song of the Lord, struggle to reach the high notes as I did before. I could have become distraught since ninety-five percent of these diseases are caused by smoking, and I have *never* smoked. But I choose to walk by faith and watch the Healer do His work.

"He sent his word and healed them and delivered them from their destructions." (Psalms 107:20, KJV)

Holistic healing is my aim, and through the avenues in which God walks on before me, I will arrive. I am not only being made whole in my mind/soul, but also in my body.

Thanking God all the way for the interventions of doctors and medicines, for He has used them many times for me. Pastor Louann has decreed and declared that one day God is going to grow me another lung, and I, along with many others, are in total agreement for this miracle.

"Thou shalt decree a thing, and it shall be established unto thee: and the light shall shine upon thy ways." (Job 22:28, KJV)

Life is always a walk of faith but do I let these new challenges stop me? I mean, if I can continue to live and write through two broken wrists, grief, lung cancer, PTSD, COPD, etc., surely I will not stop at anything. I continue to press forward fully believing that the good thing that He began in me He will perform. Yeshua Hamashiach-Jesus is Salvation, carries me and brings deliverance from these temporary evils.

"Being confident of this very thing, that he which hath begun a good work in you will perform it until the day of Jesus Christ." (Philippians 1:6, KJV)

"For our light, momentary affliction (this slight distress of the passing hour) is ever more and more abundantly preparing *and*

producing *and* achieving for us an everlasting weight of glory
[beyond all measure, excessively surpassing all comparisons
and all calculations, a vast and transcendent glory and
blessedness never to cease!]" (2 Corinthians 4:17, AMP)

It is by faith that you and I exist, trusting totally in the God of
Abraham.

"He staggered not at the promise of God through
unbelief: but was strong in faith, giving glory to God;
and being fully persuaded that, what he had promised,
he was able to perform." (Romans 4:20–21, KJV)

Challenges come on many levels and what tries to stop me in my
tracks, may not affect you, and visa-versa. No matter how you landed
in the pit of pain that you may find yourself in today, whether someone
or circumstances threw you in, or it was caused by wrong choices and
actions on your part, Jesus Christ, our Savior and Lord, will reach down
and pull you out. Let go of the pain, sickness, and wounds that try to
execute you. Move forward into a new day, a new beginning.

If you don't let your past die, it won't let you live.

Allow God to turn your scars into stars. Don't resist His work. Don't
try to stop it. Don't try to slow it down or speed it up, just ride with the
tempo of what the Holy Spirit is doing in your life and let Him keep the
pace. Your job is to trust him step-by-step.

Yes, hidden emotional pain may hurt just as much coming out, as
it did going in, but get it out and do not let the criticism of others cause
you to isolate yourself.

"[But what for that?] For I consider that the sufferings of this
present time, (this present life) are not worth being compared
with the glory that is about to be revealed to us and in us
and for us and conferred on us." (Romans 8:18, AMP)

You can move forward knowing that Adonai-the Lord God, is with you always and forever. Jehovah Shalom, He is your peace. He will give you sweet and perfect peace, for that's Who He is, our Wonderful and Mighty Prince of Peace. Peace meaning; nothing missing and nothing broken.

I have learned the meaning of love and loss in the last year of my life, *love is immovable*, and *loss is subject to change*. Jesus the Mediator, pulls our lives together, steps in and makes us whole again.

"And we know all things work together for the good to them that love God, to them that are the called according to his purpose." (Romans 8:28, KJV)

God does not waste anything, including pain. Coming to this realization I feel like I have only begun to fight the good fight of faith.

"Fight the good fight of faith, lay hold on eternal life, whereunto thou art also called, and hast professed before many witness." (1 Timothy 6:12, KJV)

Two things pierce the human heart, beauty and affliction. –– Simone Weil.

Chapter 31

~ *Nature Abhors Vacuum* ~

Today I discovered from a recent CT scan of my left lung, that my physical heart had literally shifted its given position within the petite frame of my body. There was a void in my chest cavity. This was created when the lower left lobe of my lung was surgically removed over a year ago due to cancer. "Nature abhors vacuum," the doctor said to me. What a statement.

"He that hath an ear let him hear what the Spirit is saying to the churches." (Revelation 3:6, kjv)

There is a place, an alignment of the body of Christ in the earth. The eye cannot say to the ear, "I have no need of you." Each part of us is essentially important. By God's amazing design we are fearfully and wonderfully made. When a limb is lost, say your right arm; the left arm, shoulder, elbow, even the side of your body will swing into motion to help accomplish the task at hand. So goes the body of Christ. When a member is not in proper position and not filling their rank, we feel the slack. We sense the emptiness. Seemingly all within and without the circle are affected. Have you not been in a congregation when a person, maybe youth leader, deacon, or even a pastor has fallen away? Gone in the despairing ravages of sin, and the huge painful void that is left in the wake... the hollowness, crying, grief, emptiness blankets the people. "What will we do? What's going to happen with that certain person no longer in their place?" These questions tantalize us. But over a period of gracious time, good soldiers step in, and began to bring wholeness by sliding into the vacant slots. Over time, pain is reduced and the shame is minimized. The shifting has diametrically come. You may not have even noticed *when* it happened or how but you just know that it did.

This is a necessary process. Out of love and commitment to our Lord we move accordingly by His Spirit and the change takes place. So goes the human body. My eyes were opened that day as I sat in the doctor's office. I had never even thought such a thing could or would happen inside me. My heart has shifted... wow! My mind is still rocking with this absolute. My heart has shifted slowly over a period of time into the vacant spot in my body. So slowly- I did not even realize it. It is lower now within the confines of my chest cavity. I think *lower*. My heart has bowed lower. Lower in humility. The challenges I have experienced have completely changed my outlook on life. I do not have even the slightest desire for *front and center ministry position* or *platform seating*. My heart and spirit have shifted slowly over this process, to a sweet, humble positioning in the body of Christ. To love my neighbor as I love myself, to team up with another's vision rather than my own, to give words of encouragement, to pray for someone is a lifestyle all its own. Just to be genuinely concerned with others and the obstacles they are facing; I find deeply gratifying. Releasing a gospel that's compels me to give myself away daily in the simplicity of life is rewarding.

Yes- my heart has shifted; to love and cherish the quantity of time I have with my family and my husband who has become my best friend. Yes- my heart has shifted. My children and my precious half-dozen grandchildren; whom I think I took for granted while we were all in Florida together. I let it become commonplace to have the babies playing at my feet. Living in another state far from my precious family produced an empty space inside me, but now I fully realize what treasures from heaven they really are; gifts which the Bible calls, *life's reward*.

"Lo, children are an heritage of the Lord: and the fruit of the womb is his reward." (Psalms 127:3, KJV)

Nature abhors vacuum indeed. Our soul must now move into the empty parts of this earthbound life into our daily world. Satisfy the void I say... Take time to examine your life and its content. Close up the holes, the barren spaces of your soul and survey the sphere of influence that God has afforded you.

I remember the one and only time I saw my chest x-ray about six months after the surgery. What I saw haunted me for days. To look at a picture of the inside of my body and see the empty place where the lung once lived. It seemed so wrong that it was taken from me. I cried that day feeling a sense of loss. *I was fragmented!*

It took me back to a few years earlier when my sister-in-law had an accident and one of her fingers had to be amputated. I grieved with her for several days. What seemed so unfair, struck my heart with sadness. The loss of her precious forefinger could never be replaced. What an illustration, and what a lesson I have learned.

Life is fragile, and our bodies a gift; the very temple of the Holy Spirit. We take for granted what we have until the day we no longer have it. Oh how true this is! *Nature abhors vacuum,* is a phrase I will never forget. This day has marked me. I struggle to put into writing how this has altered my personal life. I pray these closing comments bare the effects of my soul.

We are unique. There is only one of you and one of me. I have one spirit, one life to live, one mission to accomplish, one destiny to fulfill. I don't want to leave a void in the earth because I failed to make my mark. My aim is to impact every person that God ordains. May I complete my purpose, do the job, and run the race that is set before me, leaving no vacuum. I am embracing a remarkable paradigm shift. I can't tell you the day or the hour it occurred, yet I know the conversion is within me.

My desire is to plant trees of righteousness inside of people all along the voyage of my life. Let it not be said of me that I left a massive or miniscule hole anywhere in the earth. Oh, how I long to leave a legacy.

So, let us cooperate with the move of the Holy Spirit in this cultivation process I call; *living life to the fullest.* Clothe yourself with knowledge of who *He* is and of who *you* are. There is more to us than meets the eye. Prepare to fulfill the vision of God, make your calling and election sure.

There is a generation coming up behind us that we must leave a deposit in. We want no gaps in the development of their hearts and lives.

"This is the generation of them that seek Him that seek Thy face. The generation of Jacob." (Psalm 24:6, KJV)

Nature abhors vacuum, or in other words; *creation cannot tolerate empty spaces.* It despises them. God's magnificent creation whether it be man, beast, plants or trees, will not permit vacancies of any kind. What is the measure of a man? Do I proportion my heart to love? Do I fill my love gauge to its capacity? Do I give myself away and embrace the dream of God? The dream for unity and wholeness within my own body, my own family, and the body of Christ? Do I engage my spirit to love with all my heart, soul, mind, and strength?

Yes, I am grateful that my heart is learning each day to bow lower in the presence of the King, **under** the hand of the Almighty God. And I thank God that He allowed me to walk out my pain; and use that same pain, to thrust me forward into His Arms.

Every part of me desires to be in the position that He ordains, no matter how high or how low. Selah~

Chapter 32

~ *One Full Year* ~

———————∿∿∿∿∿∿∿∿∿∿———————

Exactly 1 full year, the 365 days that we were privileged to give, live, work, pray, and sing prophetically over Virginia was full indeed. Not only did the Holy Spirit reveal to me my hidden pains, which I have talked so openly about; God did a triumphant work in my soul. He hid me away on this quiet mountain and healed me from the inside out. Such detailed events of this past year could only have been orchestrated by the Holy Spirit.

Along with the privilege that God gave me to diligently give myself to prayer for the region, I was also a part of the International Outreach ministry with Pastor Louann. Additionally, I worked in the church office, taught the adult class on Wednesday nights on occasion, and helped give food in abundance to the poor. Working with Pastor Louann inspired me to pursue the dream of God. She had this saying, *if you can dream it, you can have it*. Which is simply the steps of faith. I learned that every dream has a beginning. It's like God places dream seeds inside you and your words of faith cause them to grow.

"Now faith is the substance of things hoped for and the evidence of things not seen." (Hebrews 11:1, NKJV)

Through all my turbulence this year, I continued believing for the goodness of God. This year had been rough, real and raw, but also redemptive, restoring and reviving. God let me know He was going to use everything I walked through for His glory.

On the eleventh month of our stay, the doors for our livelihood in Virginia began to close. We approached Pastors Roger and Louann and told them what was happening. They gave us the greatest nuggets of wisdom by saying, "Let the four of us pray and fast together for three days and see what God speaks to us individually. Don't make any phone calls back home to Florida in preparation to move, don't pack any boxes, just be very still and walk softly before the Lord for three days." We gladly submitted to the process.

I lay in my bed on the third day, after God had confirmed we were to return to our homeland of Florida. It came through a dream I had the night before. I woke up, and slid off my bed and onto my knees in my small bedroom; that I sometimes referred to as my cubicle.

I buried my head between my hands and from the very depths of my soul I cried, "Jesus, you said in your word that if I would leave houses and lands, and sons and daughters for your sake, and the gospel's sake, to follow You; that you would give me back one-hundred fold return in this life, and in the life to come, eternal life. You know Jesus; we no longer have a home in Florida. We gave up our house and land, left our sons and daughters, to follow You. We have no jobs, and no place to lay our head. Where in the world are we going to live?"

"Verily I say unto you, there is no man that hath left house, or brethren, or sisters, or father or mother, or wife, or children, or lands, for my sake, and the Gospel's, but he shall receive an hundredfold now in this time, houses, and brethren and sisters and mothers and children and lands, with persecution; and the world to come eternal life." (Mark 10:29-30, KJV)

I got back up on my bed and thought to call my brother Joey; who lives in Lakeland, Florida.

Quickly updating him on what I felt God was doing and saying, I asked him if we could stay with him for a few weeks until we could find the place that God would provide. Joey, knowing the life of faith that we lived, said a swift, "Yes". Shortly after his, yes, he paused, then he broke the silence with this question, "Would you want to live in

Winter Haven?" I said "Sure". Winter Haven is just two cities over from Lakeland and I thought that would be ideal. Then I said, "Why do you ask Joey?" Informingly he spoke of our mutual friends, Theda and Steve, who had a home that they were trying to sell in Winter Haven. Our friends had recently moved their lives to Tennessee, and had renters living in their home in Winter Haven. Joey said, "Let me call her, and I'll call you right back." I was on pins and needles as I waited for the return call. Twenty minutes, thirty minutes, forty minutes, fifty minutes, finally, an hour had passed when the phone rang. It was *not* Joey, but Theda. In her cute Tennessee accent, as she spoke so matter-of-factly, saying, "Okay girlfriend, I hear you're heading back to Florida. Here's what we're going to do. When you drive into Florida, go to Winter Haven to this address, there will be a lockbox with the key. Here's the number, go in the house and live there for two or three months at no expense to you. If, by the end of those two or three months, you and Phillip decide you want to live there; I will sell it to you for five." I piped up and said, "$5,000?" "Yes, $5,000", she explained. "But there's one thing I have to tell you. Everything you would ever need in a home is there. Towels, sheets in the linen closet, dishes in the cabinet, silverware in the kitchen drawer, china in the china cabinet, beds, TVs, DVD players, furniture, and oh yes, there's food in the freezer and food in the pantry too." She then proceeded to tell me that only two days prior, she was lying across her bed asking God to bring someone to buy her house. She specified that she did not want just anyone to live there. She and Steve had poured so much of their lives into it, praying in it and hosting many of our Christian friends for fellowship and time in the presence of the Lord. Theda desired someone in this home that would do the same. To care for it and allow the Holy Spirit His domain, was their ultimate desire. By the end of our conversation, my heavy heart was for I perceived that God was definitely directing me.

"The steps of a good man are ordered by the Lord: and he delights in his way." (Psalms 37:23, NKJV)

"Could this really be happening?" We hung up and I thought, "Did I hear her correctly?" It seemed too good to be true. Later, when Phillip got home from work, I excitedly told him the news. I asked him to call Theda and confirm the words she had spoken to me. As I listened to their conversation, I knew it was a done deal. There was no way we could deny God's providence in the situation.

We met with Pastors Roger and Louann that evening and told them what had transpired. They both agreed this was the wisdom of God, and verbally affirmed their blessing on Phillip and me to return back to Florida. They told us that we would be greatly missed on a personal level, but even more so in the church. On that note, we affectionately embraced, then made our exit back to our little home to prepare for the big exodus that was ahead

At the end of March, we were given an amazing celebratory benediction in front of the entire congregation. Also combined with a wonderful meal, which I jokingly referred to as the *Last Supper*.

Before the benediction was given, I was privileged to do a prophetic dance, which means; doing what the Holy Spirit moves you to do in the moment He moves you to do it. The chosen song I used spoke of the joy found in letting go of *our* own will and taking up *His*.

In the dance, I wore a lime-green and aqua-blue scarf around my neck and underneath the scarf was a lime-green necklace, which I will speak about in significant detail later. Preempting my dance, I laid every flag, banner and streamer I could find on the platform in specific order. As I was impressed by the Holy Spirit, I picked up a flag and joyously ran into the congregation and would place it in the hand of one the church members.

I would then run back to the platform, get another one, and do it again, and again, until all the flags were dispersed. I felt as if I was passing a baton of worship to the people. Hoping that my life here at, Critz Church of God, would be leaving an impressionable mark.

My finale was removing the lime-green scarf from my neck and joyfully waving it back and forth to the people signifying our departure. They were my family forever, no matter where I moved to. In this one full year; my dreams became bigger, my faith became stronger, my heart and soul became larger, my spirit became softer, and my vision became clearer, all because of serving these precious pastors and serving the congregation with Heaven's love. I would not change one day of these last 365 days; for each *one* of them changed me forever.

Chapter 33

~ *Florida/Forerunner/*
Lime Green ~

───∿∿◦◦⟲⟩◦⟨⟲◦◦∿∿───

**"Now Israel loved Joseph more than all his children,
because he was the son of his old age: and he made
him a coat of many colours." (Genesis 37:3, KJV)**

Joseph's colorful coat was distinctive, meaning; different in a way
that is easy to notice. His coat was intended to influence people. It was
very elaborate with a reddish overtone.

Color is characteristic of God. Have you ever noticed the brilliant
colors of the rainbow He used as a sign of His covenant? Heaven and
earth is full of color.

**"I'm putting my rainbow in the clouds, a sign of the covenant
between me and the Earth." (Genesis 9:14, MSG)**

I knew that my colors of red, white, and black, from the former season
in Virginia, would not carry over into the present season in Florida. As
I have spoken before, God speaks to me through colors. Psychological
studies have proven that color can dramatically affect moods, feelings
and emotions. Color is a powerful communication tool and can be used
to signal action and also cause reaction.

Just before leaving Virginia, a friend complimented me on the color
of my shirt, which displayed an outburst of florescent lime-green. I also

had a matching hairband and socks. The comment was, "Wow, I can see you very well!" Because color speaks volumes to me, I questioned my friend if he knew what the lime-green color represented. He stated that it meant, *upfront, high visibility*. My spirit heard him say, *forerunner*. Loud and irrefutable. Immediately, I thought of the forerunner of Jesus.

"In those days came John the Baptist, preaching in the wilderness of Judea, and saying, Repent ye: for the kingdom of heaven is at hand. For this is he that was spoken of the prophet Esaias, saying, The voice of one crying in the wilderness, prepare ye the way of the Lord, make his paths straight." (Matthew 3:1-3, KJV)

John the Baptist preceded the coming of Jesus by a few months. He was a voice crying in the wilderness to prepare the people for the coming of the Lord. God is raising up in these end-times, forerunners that will also precede Jesus' coming, His *second* coming. My heart resonates the call to be a forerunner declaring His return. Jesus is coming again!

"For the Lord Himself will descend from heaven with a loud cry of summons, with the shout of an archangel, and with the blast of the trumpet of God. And those who have departed this life in Christ will rise first. Then we, the living ones who remain [on the earth], shall simultaneously be caught up along with [the resurrected dead] in the clouds to meet the Lord in the air; and so always (through the eternity of the eternities) we shall be with the Lord!" (1 Thessalonians 4:16–17, AMP)

We are made to be lights in this dark world. No, you don't have to wear bright color clothing to do it, just have the light of His countenance on your face. Along with a boldness in your heart to speak openly about God.

While still in Virginia, I was shopping in a local store when my eyes were drawn to lime-green, aqua-blue plaque which read "Dream Big". If there was one thing Pastor Louann imparted into me; it was to dream and to be full of vision for the future. So the words alone first caught my attention. It was explosively lit up with vivid lime-green colors that I could not miss it. Holding the plaque, I turned and my eyes caught sight of a scarf with the identical colors and pattern. Turning once more, I noticed a lime-green hand-basket. Happily, I placed the plaque and the scarf inside the basket and began to make my way to the check-out counter. In route, an adorable lime-green piggy-bank caught my attention. I snatched it up and placed it in the basket. "What an impromptu moment," I giggled.

At home, I eagerly placed them on the living room floor, glancing at them throughout the remainder of the day. With an unexplainable happiness, I knew these were going to be the new colors that would surround me. Also these colors would be a daily reminder of who I am called to be; a voice to declare to a dark world that Jesus, the Bridegroom, is returning soon looking for a lovesick Bride. What better color could speak such volumes? After thought provoking looks, I gently placed all the articles back in the bag and moved them to the corner of the room. Later, I found myself opening the bag again and placing them on the floor. I did this about three times, until I finally decided to leave them out. As I thoroughly enjoyed their colorful illumination for hours, I dreamed of being back on the front lines again fulfilling my total destiny in ministry with complete use of my hands, my lungs and my sound mind. I finally recognized that God was putting fresh vision in my heart for the new season that was awaiting me in the same way he had done when I left Florida to move to the red cardinal State of Virginia.

Upon entering Winter Haven, Florida, we anxiously drove to our new home to see exactly what it looked like. Trembling with excitement, I grabbed my new lime-green scarf, yes, the one I danced with at our benediction, and whipped it around my neck as we walked through the door. We slowly made our way around the house looking in each adorable room. The house was a mansion compared to our tiny home on the mountain with three large bedrooms, two bathrooms, a dolled up screened-in patio, barbeque grill, big screen television, etc. Within an hour or so I tacked up the *Dream Big* plaque on the wall and artistically arranged the scarf to enshroud it. It dazzled me with fresh life and vision. I was ecstatic!

All of our children came over to greet us and welcome us back home. They wanted to help unpack what few articles we did possess. My daughter, Charity, looked in the kitchen cabinets at the dishes that came with the home; she screamed, "Mom come quick!" Carefully, she pulled the plates and bowls out for me to see. Tears of absolute joy came streaming down my face. You guessed it. They were nothing short of lime-green and aqua-blue! Delightfully, but not delicately, I wailed, "God! You are so faithful!"

These are the exact words I screamed when I came up out of the water while swimming in the Sea of Galilee, because God is so faithful.

> "God is faithful, by whom ye were called unto the fellowship of his Son Jesus Christ our Lord." (1 Corinthians 1:9, NKJV)

God's nature is to be intricately involved in the entirety of our lives. He loves us and He receives great joy when we are delighted in small things; such as a colored plate that matches what we're feeling.

He will be as perceptible as much as we can receive, not just in our ministry, but in our ordinary, everyday lives.

> "Blessed be the Lord, who daily loads us with benefits, the God of our salvation! Selah." (Psalms 68:19, NKJV)

There was a large, gorgeously carved wood dining room table in the dining room. For display, I properly placed the colorful dishes as a table setting. The more I viewed them and the scarf and plaque displayed beautifully on the living room wall, the more of God's vibrancy flowed through me. His effervescence was washing away all the death and darkness that I had walked through. It felt good to be alive!

God was using these colors to bring me into a greater awareness of my calling; to be a voice as one crying in the wilderness telling others that *Jesus is coming. Wake up your bridal love and prepare to meet your*

Bridegroom King. He's coming, get ready! I began to carve out my schedule to meet with God in intense prayer. As the colors were echoing life from the walls and tables of my home, they were regenerating the vividness of vision within my soul. It catapulted me into the spirit realm to such a degree that I was contagious with *life* and *joy.* Each time I encountered family members or friends that I had not seen over the past year, comments were made of how alive I looked, how healthy, and vibrant I was.

This is the proof that with complete trust and dedication unto the Lord, we can come out of our hot, fiery trials and not be burned. Just as the three Hebrew boys who were literally thrown in a large oven because of their stance with God. The Lord never left them, He joined them in the fire; just as He did with me. Yes, all the trials of my past travels were extremely hot, yet the fire had no power to kill me. As with the three Hebrew boys, I knew God was with me each step of the way.

> "He answered and said, Lo, I see four men loose, walking in the midst of the fire, and they have no hurt; and the form of the fourth is like the son of God." (Daniel 3:25, KJV)

After the first week in our new home, we had fallen in love with it, along with city of Winter Haven. Everything was fresh and new. Surely God has kept His word to me. He has given me back one-hundred fold since I gave Him my one-hundred fold in following Him. All my mourning had been turned into dancing, and all my sorrow had been turned into joy. The emotional trauma I dealt with in Virginia felt light-years behind me.

Just like David in Ziglag, I had recovered all. Did I mention there are not one, but two small ponds in my gated community, and we are directly across the street from a beautiful lake? For a triple beneficial blessing I regularly swim in our large community pool that sets next to the clubhouse. God never ceasing to lead this psalmist beside still water.

Riding down the roads of my newfound city, I saw a lime-green vehicle pass me. There was no way anyone could not see it. It was a PT;

Plymouth Truck, Cruiser. Just as I saw it, out of my mouth I yelled, "I want one of those! It looks like a getaway gangster car from the classical black and white movies with James Cagney and Humphrey Bogart. It's so cute. It would be like a *grandma's getaway car* for me." With my grandchildren now living in close proximity, I could use a car like this to pick them up and take them away at the drop of a hat, so we could **live, love, and laugh.** I contacted my niece, Heather, who lives in Lakeland and owns a business designing prints on clothing. I shared with her and her husband the vision I had of the car. I requested for them to make eight designer t-shirts for me, Phillip, and our six grandchildren. I wanted a lime-green PT Cruiser in the center with the words *Grandma's Getaway Gang.* Around the words were to be six bright colored circles. Each color representing one my grandchildren.

Here are my grandchildren's names, with the specific colors I chose, and what they represent:

Eden-Glory: Pink-Universal for love, says, "I will love you forever"
Gavin: Orange-Vitality, endurance, thoughtfulness and sincerity
Benjamin: Green-Life, balance, growth and master healing
Mitchell: Blue-High ideals, inspiration, heavens and oceans
Gabriel: Yellow-Pure, creative, intellectual, awareness and wisdom
Anna: Purple-Good judgment, peace, spiritual fulfillment and royalty

The shirts were made and I hung one in my laundry room on the clothes rack. It faced me every time I walked by. On purpose, I kept the vision of my dream car in front of me. Remember, *if I can dream it-I can have it.* By faith, every single time I would see a PT Cruiser, out of my mouth would come, "Thank you God for my PT cruiser. Thank you for my Grandma's getaway car."

Oh how longed to embrace my grandchildren after being away for an entire year. I yearned to impart into their young lives my love for God, and how I love to pray; to teach them of my love for Jerusalem, and impart the sincere faith by which I live.

> "I thank God, whom I serve from my forefathers with pure conscience, that without ceasing I have remembrance of thee in my prayers night and day; Greatly desiring to see thee, being mindful of thy tears, that I may be filled with joy; When *I call to remembrance the unfeigned faith that is in thee, which dwelt first in thy grandmother Lois, and thy mother Eunice;* and I am persuaded that it in the also. Wherefore I put thee in remembrance that thou stir up the gift of God, which is in thee by the putting on of my hands." (2 Timothy 1:3–6, KJV) *emphasis mine*

Spiritual gifts can transfer from generation to generation. My mother is a powerful intercessor/spiritual songwriter as well as was my grandmother. She has told me stories of when Granny would receive letters from faraway places. Those letters conveyed spiritual dreams, they had in the night. My Granny would pray and fast for several days and God would give her the interpretation, then she would write it down in a letter and send it back. She carried such a reputation of *walking with God*, that this became a common thing in her life. As a young child, through the years 1945-1965, my mother remembers Granny asking her to taste of freshly made sweet tea from a spoon. She was fasting and didn't want anything to touch her lips. It is called a life of consecration, a life set apart unto God. This is the same lifestyle I want my children and grandchildren to carry on long after I am gone.

Being apart from my family for those 365 days has made me want to spend quality time with each one and leave the imprint of Jehovah God.

"Absence makes the heart grow fonder".--Author unknown

The free flowing favor of God is splashing all our lives. We did buy the house and it is paid in full, Hallelujah! Now it was time to go looking for my dream car. Remember, I'd practically given my car away when I moved to Virginia. I have gone a very, long time without a car, always dependent on someone else to take me to any appointments. The first year without wheels was okay because I was in the physical healing process and could not drive. But as the second year rolled around it became very difficult; I was ready to get behind the steering wheel again.

With cash in hand and our designer t-shirts on, we went on a search to find a colorful PT Cruiser. A friend told me of a banana yellow PT Cruiser at a car lot and I was there within twenty-four hours to test drive it. Spontaneously, I had this amazing color contest in my mind which was bringing me copious joy. At first site, I thought this was the one and called my daughter, Charity, to tell her that Gabriel her son and my yellow baby, had won my fictitious contest. Yet after test driving this five-speed, I realized it would have been too difficult for my wrists to handle; so I walked away. I expressed to God that I would be happy with any of the colored circles on my Grandma's Getaway Gang shirt for my car. We found a purple PT Cruiser about an hour away that an individual was selling. As we drove up it looked great, I thought my little princess, Anna. But the closer I got, the more I realized this car had way too many battle scars. This was not a dream car at all. I later saw on the Internet a deep pink PT Cruiser, which was so far away and due to time restraints, were not able to make that journey. I friend from church told my husband of a site on the internet that we were not familiar with. Speedily, Phillip located a popping electric blue PT Cruiser with chrome accentuations. The picture was impressive. With money in hand, we took off again to Venice, Florida to see it. When we arrived at the owner's home, it was dark and there was no PT Cruiser anywhere in sight. I was disillusioned and my heart sank. Phillip called the buyer on the phone and she said, "I'll be right out." She stepped out with a remote in her hand and opened her garage door. We were sitting in our car in the driveway. With great anticipation we watched the large, heavy, door slowly rise. There, underneath the brightest florescent lights, shining and beaming, was the most beautiful PT Cruiser I had ever seen.

It seemed to be on showcase just for me. Quickly we loaded in the car for a test drive. My heart was singing all the way down the road! I knew, that I knew, this was the one God had picked for me. Instantaneously, I thought of little Mitchell, who was the color blue in my eyes. He won the coloring contest. Little Mitchell, who at the time of this writing is three years old, has been through some difficult times, due to the divorce of his parents. I couldn't be happier that God chose his color to bring me so much joy where there had been such sorrow. I drove my dream car all the way home in daze of delight.

The next day, I took the new car out in the bright sunshine to take a few pictures to show my friends. The shiny chrome that encircled the entire vehicle had an iridescent strip inside it. As beams of sunlight shimmered on it; the colors of the rainbow began to glisten like multi-colored glitter. Wow! I have a rainbow on my car!

Truly now in seeing this, I realize that *all* my grandchildren win! Every color was there.

How unique and how detailed is our God. Are you aware that God, our Creator, has a rainbow around His throne?

"And he that sat was to look upon like a jasper and a sardine stone: *and there was a rainbow round about the throne*, in sight like into an emerald." (Revelation 4:3, KJV) *emphasis mine*

It's amazing how the Fathers love reaches out to us personally. God is forever planting dream seeds in all of us. Water them and watch them grow.

I am called to be a blaze of illumination for God just as my children and grandchildren are, and so are you, along with your descendants. Let's get to shining!

I stand as a trophy of God's grace indeed, with His deserving praise forever on my lips.

"Bless our God, O peoples! Give him a thunderous welcome! Didn't he set us on the road to life? Didn't he keep us out the ditch? He trained us first passed us like silver through refining fires, brought us into hardscabble country, pushed us to our very limit, road tested us inside and out, took us to hell and back; finally he brought us to this well-watered place." (Psalms 66:8–12, MSG)

I have only just begun to live!

Dream come true!

Chapter 34

~ *Finishing Touches* ~

Oh, the mystery and majesty of intercession! As we give ourselves to the call of praying for the world, it's funny, He sends us there. You **go** where you **sow.**

In this final chapter, please allow me to apply the finishing touches that God has placed recently on my life; conveying prophetic words that I have received through several authentic intercessors:

1. You will fly to Israel and beyond. There is a birthing, you will step into a new office, and there will be a new mantle.

2. I see hundreds of hundreds of thousands of people being changed, healed, and transformed, some of dark skin as in another nation. *As this person was speaking they grabbed hold of my wrists and continued,* as you step foot onto platforms to speak, the enemy will tremble at the anointing of God. The devil will not flee at first. God is going to make him watch with what he meant for evil with my wrists, how God has turned it for my good. *Now squeezing my wrist forcefully* said, when you play the piano the power of God will saturate the people. The enemy put a cup of poison up to your lips, but you would not drink his poison. You have kept yourself pure and God has kept the sanity of your soul. Where the devil came with sickness, disease, and pain, the Lord

that has rebuked him! The same hands that were hurt, God will now use them to pull lives out of the kingdom of darkness.

3. You have been brought into the Kingdom for such a time as this. He is renewing your strength as a twenty-year-old so you can run with His song and His word to set the captives free. You must record the prophetic sounds that come forth, for you are not a copy, you are an original. You will not be called a repairer of the breach, but a *repairer of the mind*. I see you repairing the souls of God's people.

4. God has made you a firebrand; you will burn bright as you run across the earth.

5. Go, rescue His people from the gates of hell! People are deep in darkness, deception, generational curses, and don't even know it. People's lives will never be the same because you have imparted what God has giving you. Run! Janet Run!

A life soaked in prayer and in the divine presence of God, is a life that can change people, shift atmospheres, and shake nations. This anointing is not for a select few, but for all who will yield themselves into the Master's Hands. By the Holy Spirit, that we can violently tear down the kingdom of darkness and bring in the kingdom of Light.

> "And from the days of John the Baptist until now the kingdom of heaven suffers violence, and the violent take it by force." (Matthew 11:12, NKJV)

We must be courageous enough to leave the imprint of Heaven everywhere we go.

My story, which you hold in your hand now, has been a pervasive clashing of the swords before stepping off the cliff into my destiny. Souls need what I have to give, and souls need what *you* have to give too. The world is waiting to hear the testimonies of lives just like mine that have radically been touched by God. There is a lost and dying world out there. People need Jesus in their lives; He is reality, and He is their only Hope.

Given the luxury from Heaven in seeing the world through His eyes while in Israel; my eyes are now open to see the Earth's condition and my ears hear the cries of the people. America, India, France, Uganda, Hungary and of course Israel, are just a few that are calling my name. I consecrate myself to be a true and living house of prayer, keeping the promise I made to God that day at the prayer conference, when I said, "If I didn't have a public job, I would spend my days in prayer." This venue is what will cause the needed transformation in our lives and those around us.

"And that day will I raise up the tabernacle of David that is falling, and close up the breaches thereof; and I will raise up his ruins, and I will build it. As in the days of old." (Amos 9:11, KJV)

Truly the *Tabernacle of David* is a place of worship and intercession that God has ordained. There will never be a successful, corporate, house of prayer without individuals becoming a house of prayer first. I adjure you to reach for that place with all your heart. Pray for your neighbors, family, and friends along with remembering God's chosen people. The Lord wants to plant compassion and passion in your life for things that may be greater than you can even conceive; through prayer you can go there first, then time and events begin to unveil more of His supernatural works. Don't try ride the wave of my passion, or anyone else, develop the one God has placed in you.

"But I have raised you up for this very purpose, that I might show you my power and that my name might be proclaimed in all the earth." (Exodus 9:16, NIV)

He may just call you to be a witness to the world, come, and join me, as I run to the nations!

"Pray for the peace of Jerusalem. They shall prosper that love thee. Peace be within thy walls, and prosperity within thy palaces. For my brother and companions' sake, I will now say, peace be within thee." (Psalms 122: 6–7, KJV)

In conclusion, I hope this book brings delight to the depressed, insight to the ignorant, joy to the joyless, hope to the hopeless, mercy to the misfortunate, dignity to the dying, victory to the vice-gripped, a song to the sad, grace to the grumbler, blessings to those bowed low, faith to the fearful, justice to the juror, and holiness to the humble. I pray it stirs the stagnant, gives prosperity to the people, gives knowledge to the noble, love to the loveless, and brings salvation to the sinner.

Epilogue

I have draped my heart and soul over this book, and my return has been tremendously cathartic as you can imagine. As I have walked intimately with *the Truth*, Who is the Messiah; that same Truth in telling my story has propelled me into divine purpose and destiny. Now that you have sojourned with me, my hope is that, through prayer, you find your moments of destiny, and healing; conclusively causing you to not be afraid to step out and go beyond the limitations that harmful circumstances may have brought you. It may not be easy, it wasn't for me, but it was possible. You may encounter people who don't approve of you, or what God is doing in your life, but you will discover that the people, who reject you are those who need you the most.

As King David discovered, when God gets ready to expand you, He gives you a battle first. I have a whole new concept of trials and victories since I dealt with my situations.

Part of this enlightenment came through the *servant heart* that Louann Moore had for me, which displayed how much easier life is when you have a covenant friend.

During my time in Jerusalem with her, God has wonderfully knit our hearts together as Jonathan and David.

"And it came to pass, when he had made and end of speaking unto Saul that the soul of Jonathan was knit with the soul of David, and Jonathan loved him as his own soul." (Samuel 18:1, KJV)

The lady that obeyed God *in that instant,* and sowed financially into my life to make the trip to Jerusalem possible; met me face to face two years after I returned from Israel. She has since become a member of my staff and a life-long friend. Our loving Heavenly Father will place special people in our lives, for He is El Shaddai, the One who brings all sufficiency. Trust Him to provide the right connections in your life. Then open up to discover your own catharsis, whether it is writing, singing, dancing, or simply praying… you can be free if you want to be!

"What a long time it can take to become
the person you have always been."
––Parker Palmer

Because your valleys are deeper, you will find that mountains are higher, rivers are wider, and victory is sweeter. As for me, I am healed, I am whole, my mind is alert, I am singing, playing the keyboard, praying daily, writing new books, ministering across the nation, and anticipating more international travels.

I am living, loving, and laughing with my family and friends, and waiting for my new grandbaby to arrive… Life is full and getting fuller! I am completely happy and in love with life and even more so in love with Jesus.

Life is waiting for you to live it. Healing and wholeness are at your front door, open it, and let God walk hand in hand with you. He is your every breath, your every step. He delights in showing Himself strong on your behalf. He loves you with an everlasting and unconditional love. The Great Redeemer is waiting to redeem you and set you on a new path heading toward great joy and fulfillment. Go ahead, open the door.

Afterword

If I have a hero, I would have to say it is my wife. Seeing what she has endured the last few years would have ruined a casual Christian.

From breaking both of her wrists at the same time and having surgery on them, just weeks before her planned trip to Jerusalem to minister in prayer and song from the keyboard. Shortly after-word she was diagnosed with lung cancer with the shock of losing the lower left lobe of her lung. I lived with her in helpless situations and yet she continued to keep her faith in God, and trust Him with her recovery. She has earnestly stayed in the word of God and in prayer daily. I believe all the 'knee-time' and 'word-time' kept her through these horrific trials. She never gave up, or gave an inkling as to wanting too. I literally felt her pain at times as it was hard to see her go through it. I went to bed many nights with a heaviness in my heart and a tear stained pillow, crying for my dear wife, asking God to relieve her of this great pain. God is so faithful, that is why I thank Him daily for what he has done for her. Janet started writing her manuscript shortly after the cancer. There would be many times her writing would come to a halt because of pain, weakness, and sickness. When Janet received the diagnoses of Clinical Depression and PTSD, she almost gave up on the book. Yet again, God came and lifted her as she abandoned herself to Him. Janet knew that people needed to hear her complete story; so, with noting hidden, she picked it up again.

This book I believe will literally set people free from their trials and burdens. It is good to know that there are real people with real problems out there and as they totally trust in God, He comes through for them; Janet is one of them. By choice, Janet gets very personal in this book, to help others that are struggling with life's situations that come their way. So let this true life story touch yours, and then share it with someone else. Be blessed and encouraged, by reading what The Lord, our Faithful God, has done for my wife. It is a great inspirational story that will motivate you to trust in God more than ever.

As the husband, I can't begin to tell you the pain and agony we both went through during these trying times. But I can say, that going through them have made us stronger and closer than ever. We were stretched beyond our imagination. My wife and I both have a heart for people going through their own dark days. Just trust God like we did, and see what he will do.

"God we thank You for allowing this testimony to travel all over the world to help set your people free! We give you all the glory for what you have done and continue to do."

From the husband of the author --Phillip *Flip* Penney.

Author's Page

Being the originator of this written work, Janet Penney has left no stone unturned in her story. She is passionate in recording her meticulous thoughts on paper; whether it be in a magazine article, a song, a poem, or a book.

As a young teen-ager, she penned her first song while walking through a very traumatizing time in her life.

Later as a young mother, Janet wrote a mini-book called, *The Greatest of these is Charity*; the stimulating story of when her doctor found two heart beats during pregnancy. Ecstatically, Janet planned to name the twins, *Faith and Hope*. She lay despondent in the hospital at the birth of *one* little girl; until she heard the voice of God say, "Now abides faith, hope, and charity, but the greatest of these is charity." Which is her daughters lovely name.

Janet's talented writings will move you, creatively granting you passage inside the pages of her heart.

In her upcoming book, *Olive Plants around My Table-One Family's Account of Undisputable Christian Living*; you will glean comprehensive insight into an interwoven, godly family lifestyle. Included will be narratives from their grown children; comprised with motivating manly viewpoints that can only come from Janet's husband and best friend, Phillip, the father of their children.

Look for the release of this *family-inspiring* book in the fall of 2015.

Scripture Quotations

KJV- King James Version-Henderson Publishers Marketing, LLC Peabody Ma tenth printing 2012

NKJV-New King James Version- Online Bible Gateway

NIV-New International Version-Holy Bible, copyright 1973, 1978, 1984, 2011, by Biblica

NIRV- New International Reader's Version-Holy Bible, copyright 1987 by Thomas Nelson Inc

MSG- Message Bible- Copyright 1993, 1995, 1996, 2000, 2002 by Eugene H. Peterson

AMP- Amplified Bible-Copyright 1954, 1958, 1962, 1965, 1987 by the Lockman Foundation

Bibliography

Chapter 7
Arrival-
　To Him Who Sits on the Throne- recorded by Don Moen. 1992, on the album Worship with Don Moen-Integrity/Hosanna Music.

Chapter 20
Quantum Leap or Casual Stance-
　Casual Christian-recorded by DeGarmo and Key, 1992, on the album Degarmo and Key Collections.

Chapter 27
Fire of Delay/Blind-sided by Cancer-
　Fire of Delayed Answers-written by Bob Sorge. Copyright 1996, Oasis House, Kansas City, Missouri.

Chapter 33
Florida/Forerunner/Lime Green
　Melissa Sumner Hale @ New Life Photography
　Vicarious Clothing.etsy.com
　Ian and Heather Vibbert

All definitions from-Merriam-Webster's Online Dictionary and Thesaurus, established 1996. Parent company-Encyclopedia Britannica

Merriam-Webster Online Dictionary and Thesaurus established in 1996. Parent company Encyclopedia Britannica

~~~~~~

> "And further, by these, my son, be admonished; of making many books there is no end; and much study is weariness to the flesh." (Ecclesiastes 12:12, KJV)

~~~~~~

It is finished!!!!!

To book Janet Penney for speaking engagements please contact at watchmanjkp@yahoo.com